Parasol unit
foundation for contemporary art

Goin'
Down,
Down,
Down:
Matthew Ronay

Foreword

The year 2000 began not only a new century but also a new
millennium, and with it came a revival of hope and the promise
of renewed vitality and a reinvigorated intellectual and moral
evolution. Instead of which, the last few years have seen ever-
increasing self-indulgence, lavish materialism, and a growing
laxity in moral and sexual behaviour. Facing this quandary
in our search for meaning, almost inevitably leads us to recon-
sider what Nietzsche, as early as the 1880s, predicted as
nihilism, that is the dissolution of all morality, spiritual integrity
and belief in high art.

Anyone in the art world will know that it was Marcel
Duchamp (1887–1968) who playfully heralded the advent of
nihilism and meaningless in art by boldly exhibiting a urinal as
an art object. Indeed, ever since then nihilism in art has chal-
lenged the paradigm into which it was born. Today, concepts
such as nihilism, provocation, banality, and vanity are not only
accepted in art but even expected of it. We can neither avoid
such thoughts nor ignore them – they have become integral to
our life, time and culture, and artists who deal with such
issues do so with alarming intensity and breathtaking indifference. Since what they so forcefully express both reflects our
culture and has become a part of it, we need to acknowledge
them and try to understand and respond to what they do.

Matthew Ronay's work exemplifies this state of mind.
He formulates his own response to the values and culture
of his time with such wit, clarity and directness that his work
irresistibly demands our response. I took great pleasure in
collaborating with Matthew for this, his first institutional exhibition and publication. Matthew Ronay's unfailing interest and
enthusiasm throughout our preparation for the exhibition has
been a refreshing experience that I would not have wanted to
miss. In addition to showing some of his existing works,
Matthew eagerly took the time to execute three new and large
pieces for this exhibition. Each of these works addresses a
different issue and together they announce a new departure in

his creative output. I cannot thank Matthew enough for his extraordinary commitment.

This exhibition at the Parasol unit could never have become a reality without the generosity of the lenders, who agreed to part with their works for the duration of the exhibition. I am grateful to all of them for their kindness.

Andrea Rosen, Marta Moriarty, Marc Foxx and Jordan Bastien were all a great support in securing various loans and in providing us with limitless amounts of information. For their unstinting assistance, they have my heartfelt thanks.

For this monograph, Bruce Hainley has written on Matthew Ronay's work with great insight and wit; and Michael Glover, who willingly interviewed the artist, has given us a clear sense of the person and his work. To both of them I present my heartfelt thanks.

Helen Wire has, as usual, applied her editing skills, sharp mind and vigour to contribute to another special publication. I am indebted to her for her patience and gracefully presented suggestions.

Marc Kappeler and Markus Reichenbach embarked on another odyssey of creating imaginative layouts and providing Matthew and me with countless design possibilities. I cannot thank them enough for their patience and sense of humour.

My small team at Parasol have, as always, been my backbone in this project and I would like to thank them all once more for their constant assistance.

Ziba de Weck Ardalan
Director/Curator

Foreword

Goin'
Down,
Down,
Down

Ziba de Weck Ardalan

*I like to think of the end of an era as something sexually reversed
and disturbing. A loosening of morals and ethics is a symptom
of the end, but the end is exponential and so exciting.*[1]

I first saw Matthew Ronay's work in his solo exhibition at the
Andrea Rosen Gallery, New York, in March 2005. Strewn across
the entire gallery floor were small, toy-like objects painted in
bright, often primary, colours. Their form and vivid colours con-
jured up an ideal, almost child-like, world and endowed them
with a startling energy together with a kind of naughty 'come
and get me' look that commanded the attention and possible
participation of every visitor. Yet there was nothing emotional
about them – nothing celebratory or sad. Even the disjointed
body parts lying on the floor exuded a certain indifference and
coldness reminiscent of the dismembered mannequin body
parts used by Hans Bellmer (1902–1975). But any likeness to
Bellmer's work ends there, because apart from their formal
similarity there is little connection between Ronay's work and
Surrealism. Ronay's work stems from life – its socio-political
and cultural components along with some of its more absurd
aspects – whereas Surrealist art was primarily rooted in
the dream world, within the realm of imagination and the sub-
conscious.

The exhibition was entitled *It's an Uprising!* Did this mean
the artist was expressing his anger about some issue? Was it

1   Ronay Matthew in conver-
sation with Brandon Stosuy,
The Believer, December 2005–
January 2006, p. 69.

the aftermath of an orgy, or a riot? Probably not. I was not even sure that the exhibition title was relevant to the content of the work, but predominant in the installation was an air of indifference, and unfettered directness. Since the work required my closer attention, I knelt down to examine these small objects one by one. Only then did I gradually begin to see the difference between what these pieces appeared to be and what in reality they could suggest. These objects which were clearly indifferent to me were at the same time not wholly objective.

In his late twenties then and now only 30, Ronay interprets the world in an introverted, imaginative and hyper-realistic manner. For as long as he has been making art, Ronay has also been playing music, and is currently one half of a two-man band. Over the past decade or so Ronay has also developed an increasingly insatiable appetite for the kind of innovative books and writings that have always defied the usual definitions – in particular, the writings of Raymond Queneau (1903–1976) and Georges Perec (1936–1982), both of the OuLiPo group; the post-war nouveau-roman writers Alain Robbe-Grillet (1922–) and Nathalie Sarraute (1900–1999); and pre-nouveau roman writing, such as that of Raymond Roussel (1877–1933).[2] But to return to his artistic output, one can well imagine Ronay has a long career ahead of him, having already made his mark in his own personal language of the 'unusual'.

The universe in which Ronay's mind operates has much in common with those of his favourite writers. His work is usually devoid of any conventional concept of a coherent narrative, time, or characters. In some ways, as in the writings of the nouveau-roman writers, such as Alain Robbe-Grillet, Ronay is engaged in making depersonalised objects, without alluding to any psychological aspects in them. This seems to add up to a particular vision, a way of seeing and rendering reality specific to American artists, something which Barbara Novak aptly describes as: '…the unique relation of object to idea that characterizes much of American realism from colonial times to present'.[3] Or with the sensibility of a 'maker' rather than a 'matcher' that has influenced the vision of American artists

even post World War II, from the Pop artists to Jeff Koons
(1955–), David Salle (1952–) and Paul McCarthy (1945–). With
Ronay's work this results in the need for viewer participation,
without which the experience of living through the work remains
incomplete. In other words, Ronay's objects are what they
are, while also being not what they seem to be at first glance.

In my first visit to Ronay's studio, I was confronted by a
flat, life-size, cut-out depiction of a group of hanging men,
Falling… Spilling… Sprawling… [p. 92]. All but one of the men
are fully dressed but with their penis visible, hanging outside
their trousers. Ronay told me that like most of his works they
were made out of MDF (medium density fibreboard) and
that he was making them for his solo show at the Marc Foxx
Gallery in Los Angeles in September 2005. The rest of the
works had yet to be made, but they would include among others
a simplified landscape, a display of erect mushroom-like
phalluses, a used condom hanging over a blue hula hoop, and
a row of hamburgers placed on a curved belt – a disparate
group of objects drawn from everyday life [pp. 90, 95, 97, 104].
The sustained use of pink flesh tones was noticeable and
clearly alluded to something in Ronay's mind other than to the
mere aftermath of a sex orgy. There's a morbidity about the
work that seems to presage disaster, male emasculation, and
ultimately the end of human race.

The messy world depicted by Ronay, perhaps pessimisti-
cally, is matter-of-factly presented, stripped of all feeling
and emotion, and plays too with a nihilistic state of mind. Yet
Ronay's nihilism is of a different nature to that we know from
Friedrich Wilhelm Nietzsche (1844–1900). Nietzsche, deeply and

2 OuLiPo (*Ouvroir de Litté-
rature Potentielle*, or Workshop
of Potential Literature), a
Paris-based group of writers
founded in 1960 by Raymond
Queneau and François
LeLionnais.

3 Novak, Barbara, *American
Painting of the Nineteenth
Century*, New York: Harper &
Row, Publishers, pp. 15 and
19, 1979.

emotionally engaged in his beliefs, was convinced European culture and Christian society were facing a major human crisis and that there would come a time of deepest self-reflection. Other thinkers and writers, who followed Nietzsche in his view and assessment of society – such as Jean-Paul Sartre (1905–1980) and Albert Camus (1913–1960) in France, and Martin Heidegger (1889–1976) and Karl Jaspers (1883–1969) in Germany – no longer considered this a disastrous condition, but rather saw it as a positive affirmation of life if one was able to confront it.

Throughout the history of twentieth-century art there has been a preoccupation with meaninglessness and absurdity. Marcel Duchamp (1887–1968) indulged in the provocative act of exhibiting a urinal and a bottle rack as art, much as in 1916 young exiles, such as Tristan Tzara (1896–1963), Hugo Ball (1886–1927) and others disillusioned with a society paralyzed by war, delighted in initiating the nihilistic Dada movement. Since then, one generation of artists after another has taken on the challenge of nihilism and absurdity and dealt with it in a variety of ways, and today the ease with which contemporary artists and writers deal with the concept of nihilism has sur-passed all expectation.

In her most interesting book *The Banalization of Nihilism*, Karen L. Carr elaborates on the concept and development of nihilism from Nietzsche to the present, and writes: '…what in fact has happened in the last two decades is a recasting of the problem of nihilism into a framework so different from that shared by Nietzsche and his unwitting successors that the work of these earlier thinkers is in danger of becoming unintel-ligible.' And she concludes by saying: 'Nihilism, the bane of the nineteenth century, is fast becoming the banality of the late twentieth century. The loss of truth prophesied by Nietzsche, has become reality in post-modern circles, yet without the attendant loss of meaning he also predicted. In the post-modern world, we can have meaning without truth because we can have knowledge without truth. The nineteenth-century belief that if truth disappeared, so too must knowledge and meaning, has become supplanted; in a world without truth (it is held) both knowledge and meaning still abound.'[4]

Just as it is not difficult to understand the sex-death connection which Ronay makes in his work *Falling... Spilling... Sprawling...*, it is easy to understand Ronay's disillusionment with the world, with its propensity for war, the Iraq war, any war, and in particular the American strategy of war – the fact that the US is increasingly perceived as a potential threat to the rest of the world. What is Ronay's perception of the war in Iraq? Does he see a way out of this dead end? Ronay is a man of his time and like most Americans of his generation he can no longer believe in American supremacy nor in his country as the land of promise. In his work Ronay continually challenges America's role as the guardian of the world. For his exhibition *Oh My God What Are We Gonna Do?!* at Vacio 9 Gallery, Madrid, in February 2006, Ronay took up the issue of the American war in Iraq and reverted to the hippie motto 'Make love, not war', except that what Ronay prescribes is lovemaking among soldiers: 'If soldiers are pushed to become gay, there would possibly be a sex orgy at the beginning, but slowly they would start loving one another instead of killing,' Ronay suggested as we talked about his work. How convincing all this is, I cannot judge, but that certainly sounds a better option than making war.

There is surely also an element of narcissism in Ronay's work. After all, narcissism is of our time and in a way not foreign to human vanity and the fear of mortality. Looking at the young, almost naked soldier/body-builder relaxing on the beach in *Medevac Flashback...Therapy Anal Leakage* [p. 87] we know he is strong, magnificent, and possibly still believes in his own immortality. In *Please Don't Bend, Fold, Spindle or Mutilate Me* [p. 86] the lean and muscular trunk of a black male hangs

4   Carr, Karen L. *The Banalization of Nihilism*, Albany: State University of New York Press, pp. 5 and 140, 1992.

from the ceiling and is about to crush a woman, whose open mouth pleads for mercy. Then in *Ground Surveillance Love Fruition with Farticles* [p. 80] two male figures, probably soldiers, hide behind the trees in a park. The lush green space of the military compound is beautiful and the white fence keeps at bay the enemy – the Iraqi population that American soldiers are bombing. This is an idyllic world in which to engage in love-making, a sort of Island of Cythera? Indeed, a recurrent theme in Ronay's work seems to be male-and-male imagery, which he sees as the new object of desire in our time.

I have talked about an uprising, about a group of hanging men, about war, about gay sex among soldiers, all of which seem to conjure up threat and danger in what is a pretty unpleasant world. Yet Ronay's work is rooted in the reality of life, and often takes the form of a stage on which the theatre of life is laid bare. He usually works to a large scale, at least life-size, for his works and frequently uses primary colours to paint his objects. Even his working method is rooted in the traditional Western art of object making. To create his three-dimensional pieces Ronay always starts with drawings. He uses wood – albeit MDF, a cheaper version – to make his objects, then he paints them, just as many generations of object-makers have done before him. All this he needs to do himself, scrupulously, without the help of any assistant. Yet it is in the ideas and vision that Ronay's work defies convention. Ronay's vision of the world in which he lives is rather grim, but just as Nietzsche nevertheless believed that nihilism had within it the possibility for redemption, Ronay also thinks the self-extermination we are all facing is only the end of an era. One senses this when he says: 'But really, people are amazing, and I want to get into them. There is only so much of your own kind that you can get into.'[5]

5   Ronay Matthew in conversation with Brandon Stosuy, *The Believer*, December 2005–January 2006, p. 76.

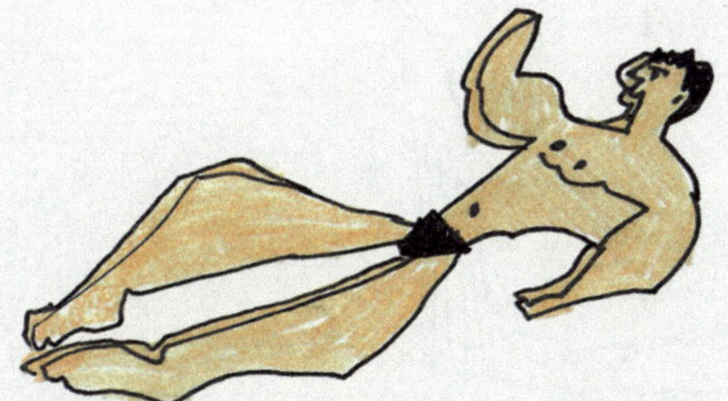

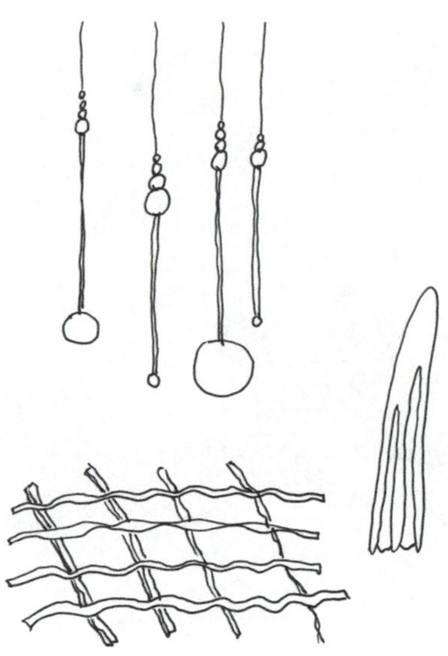

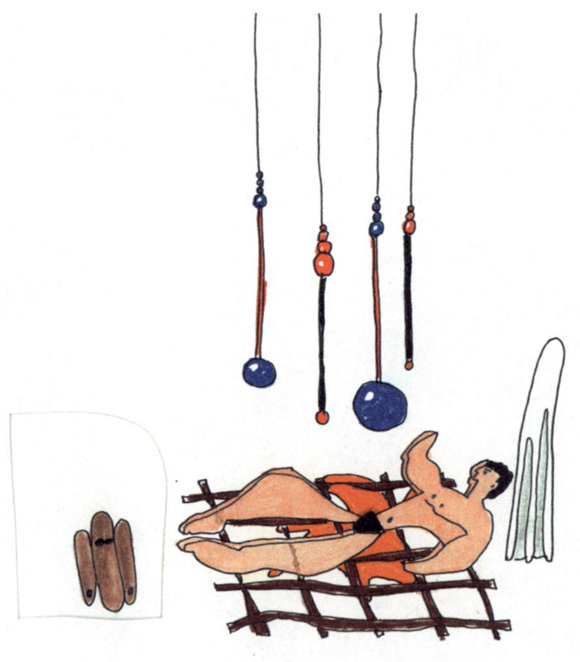

    b c

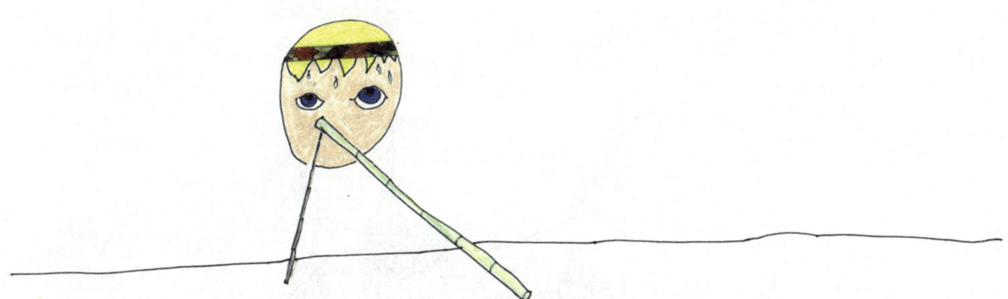

d

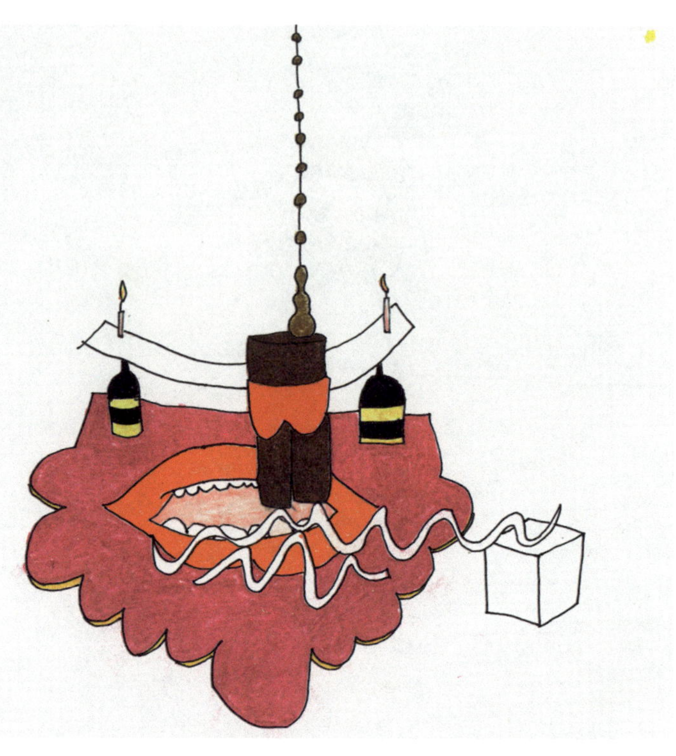

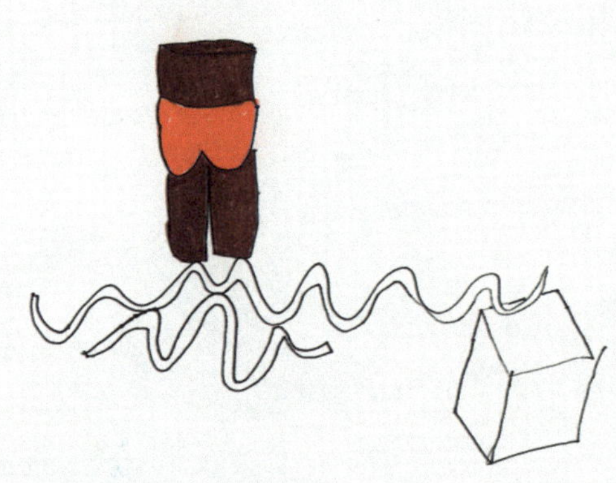

20   e f

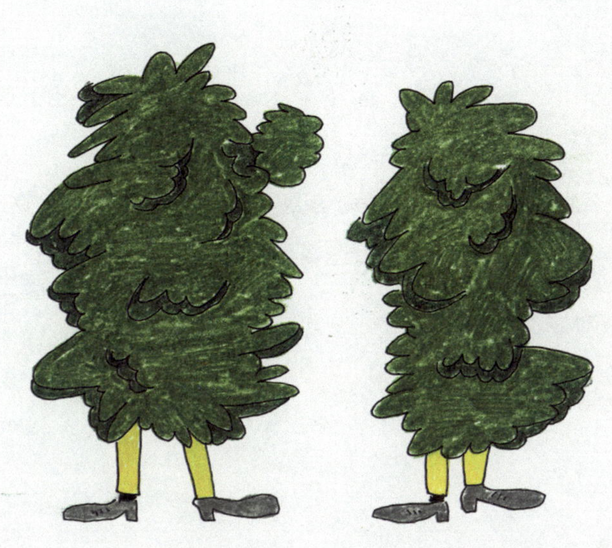

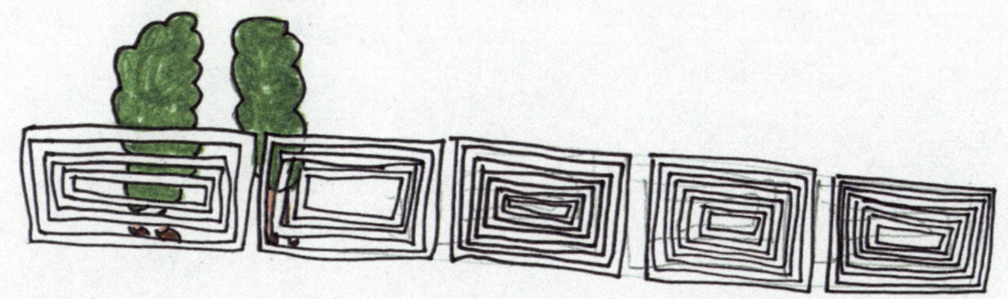

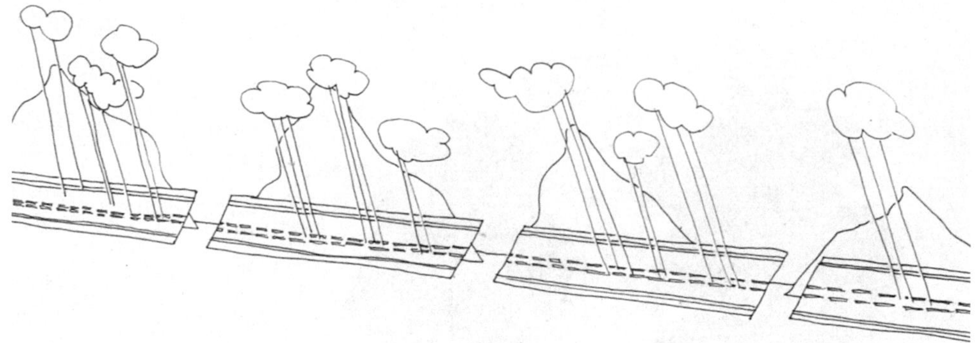

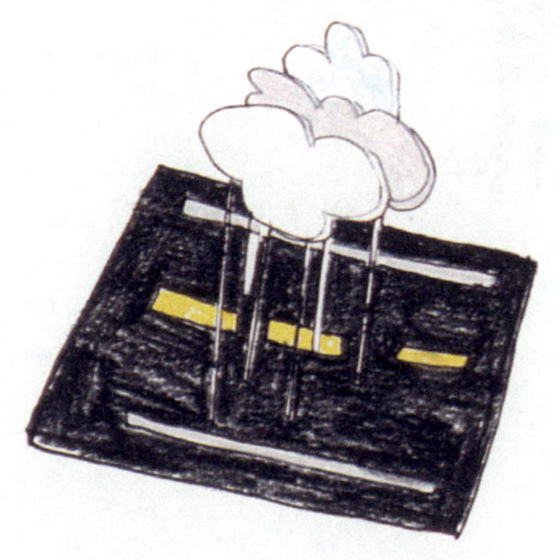

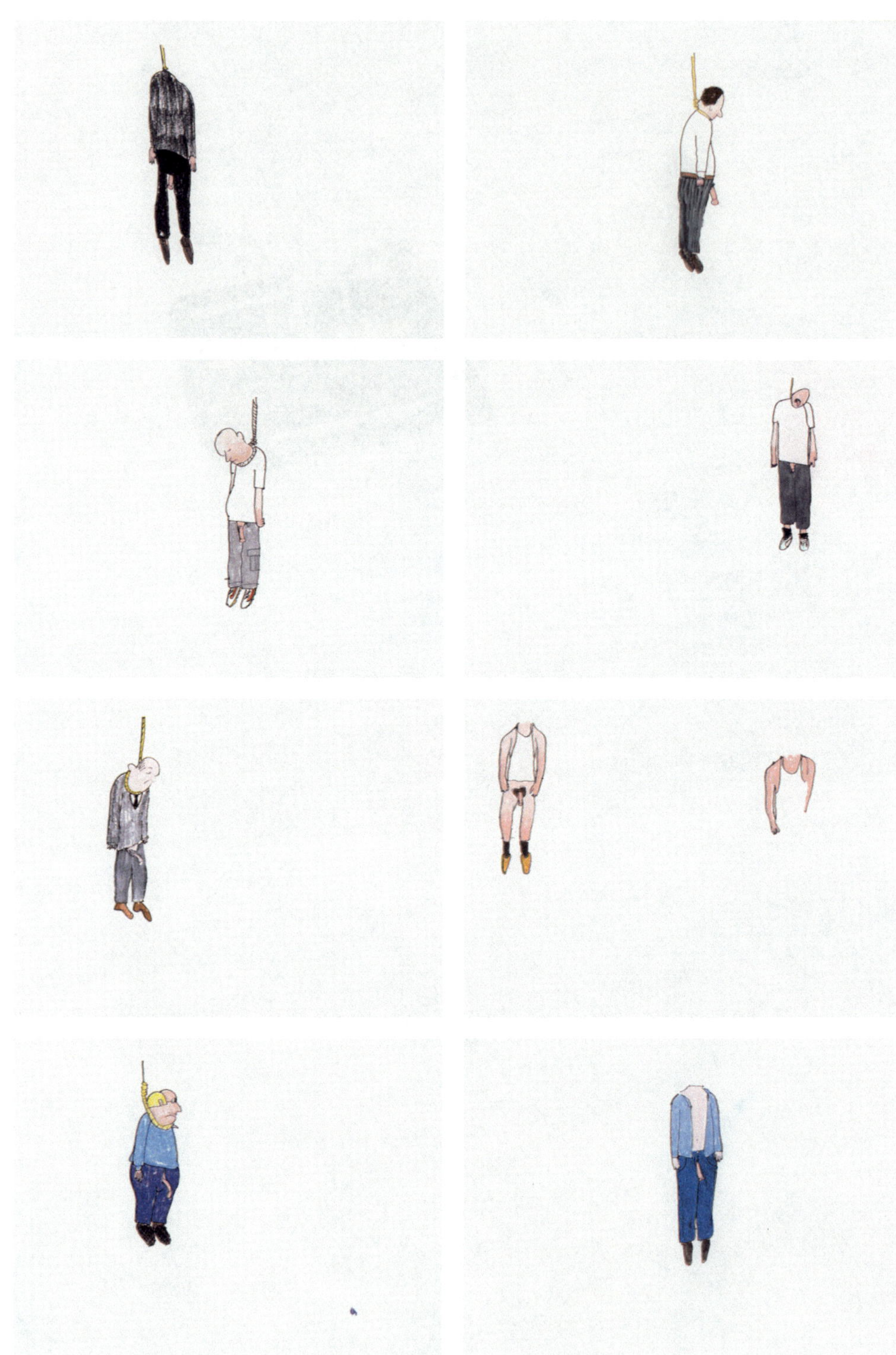

     k1 k2 k3 k4   k5 k6 k7 k8

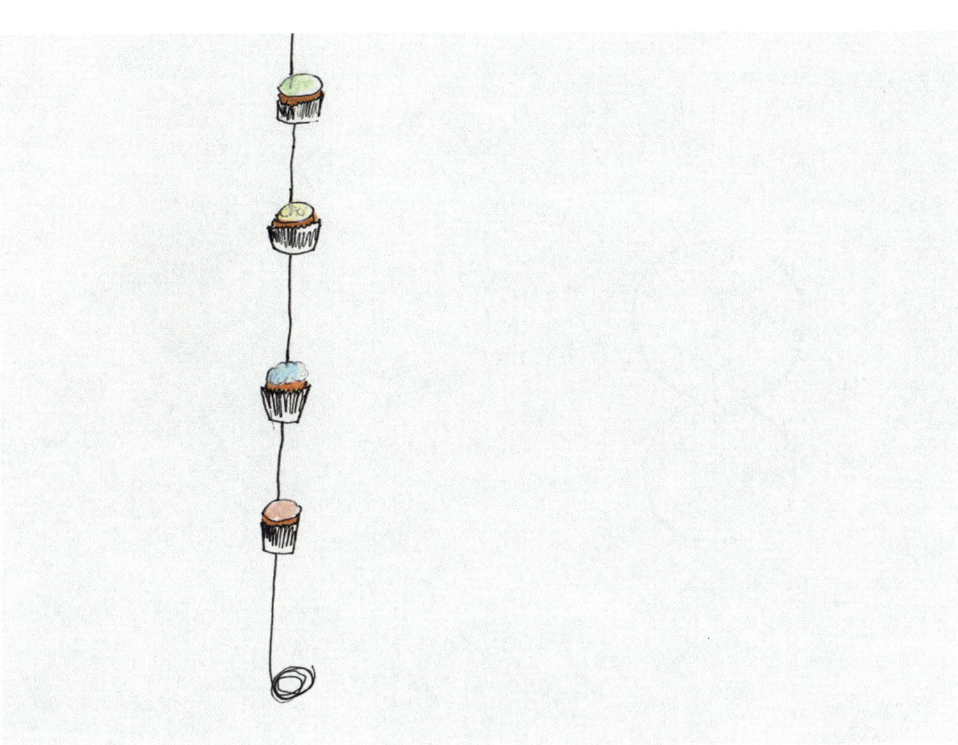

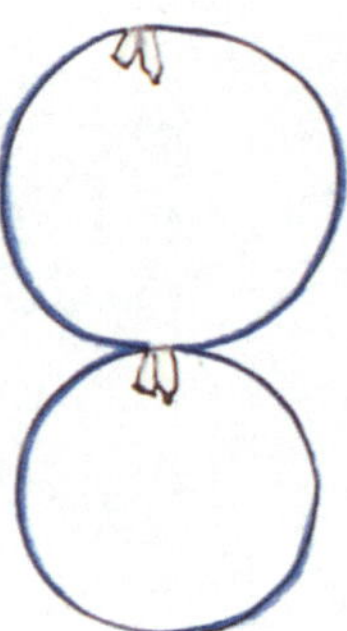

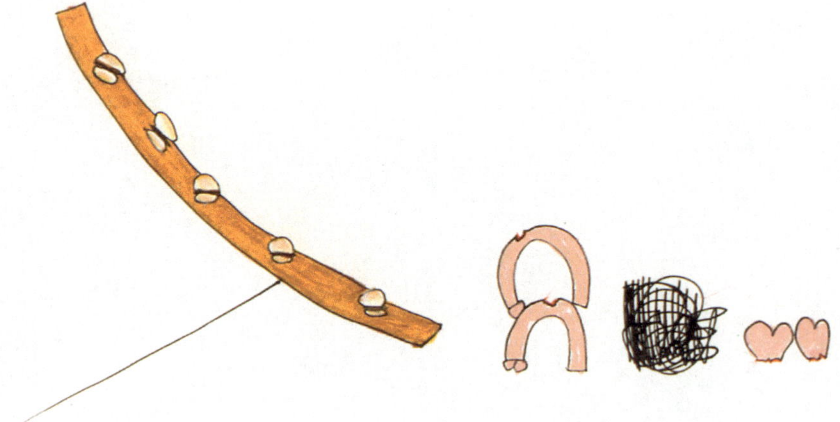

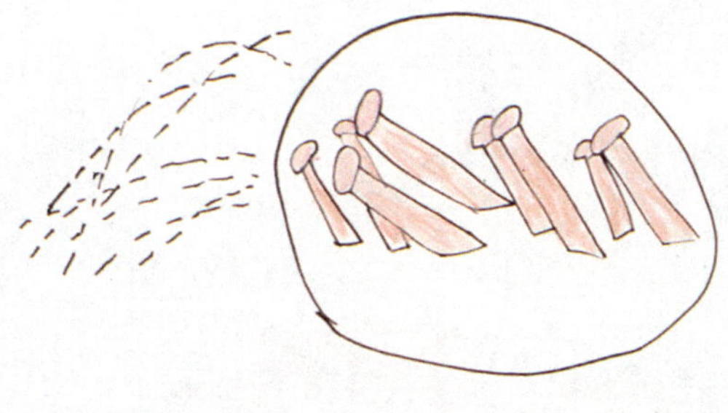

o

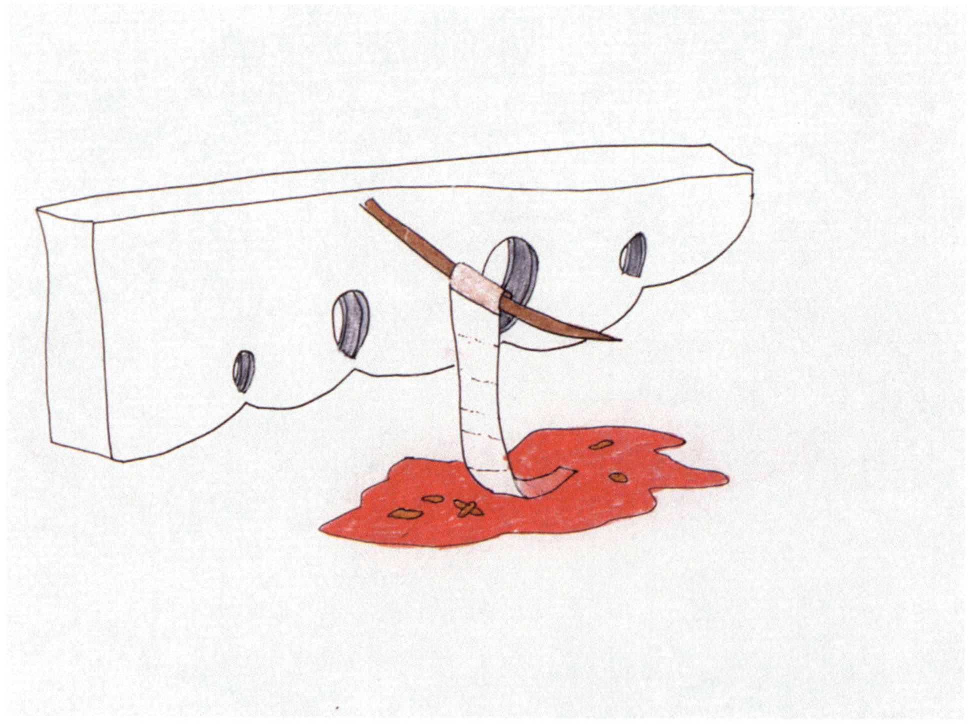

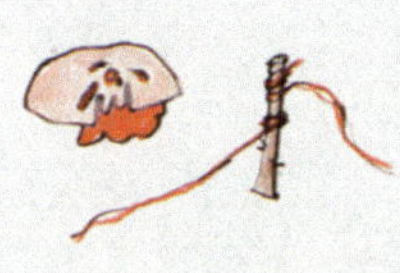

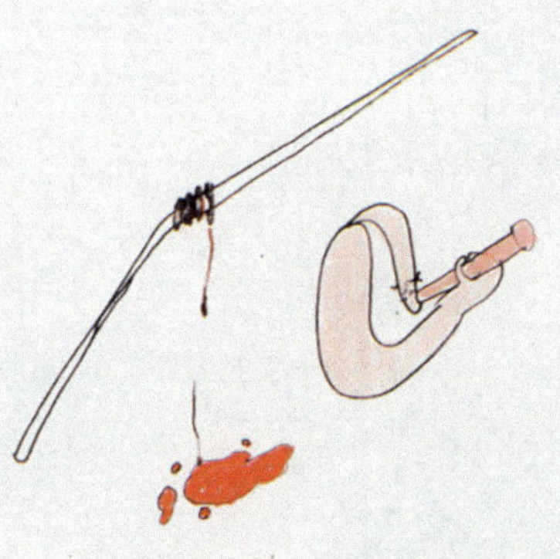

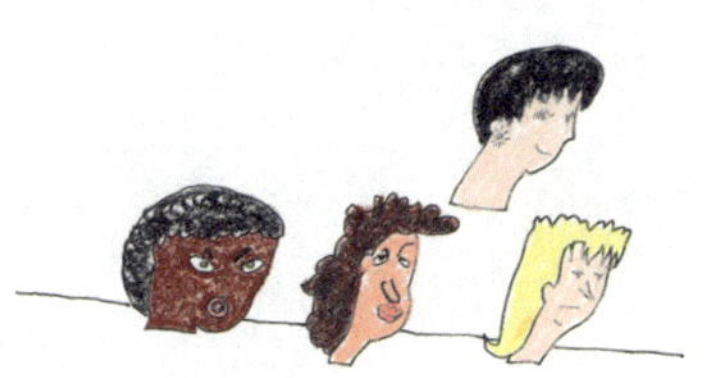

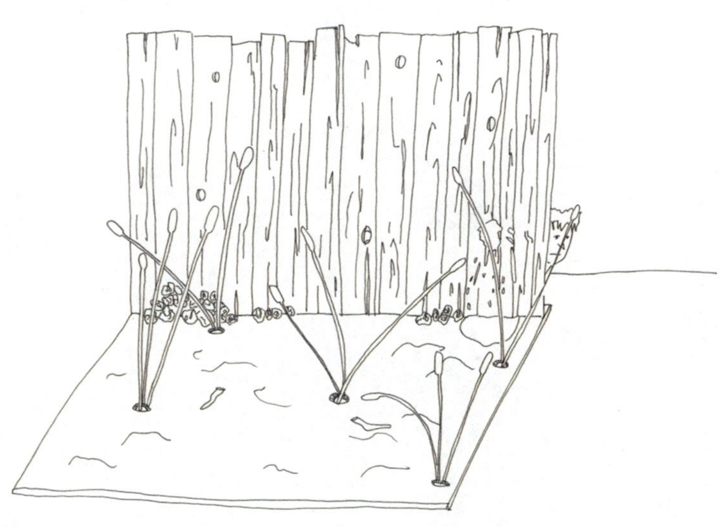

s t

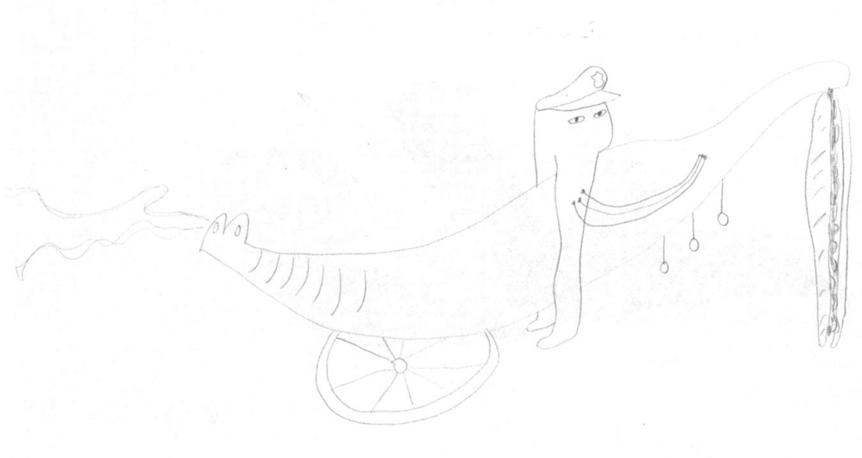

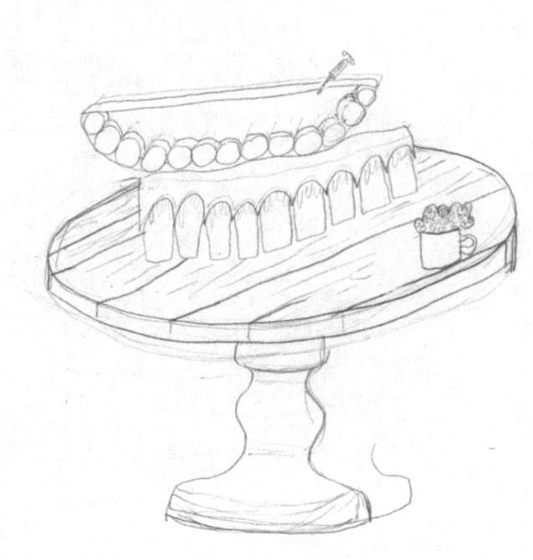

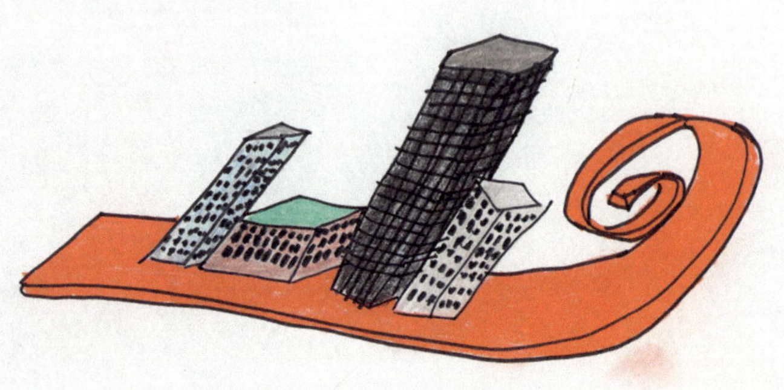

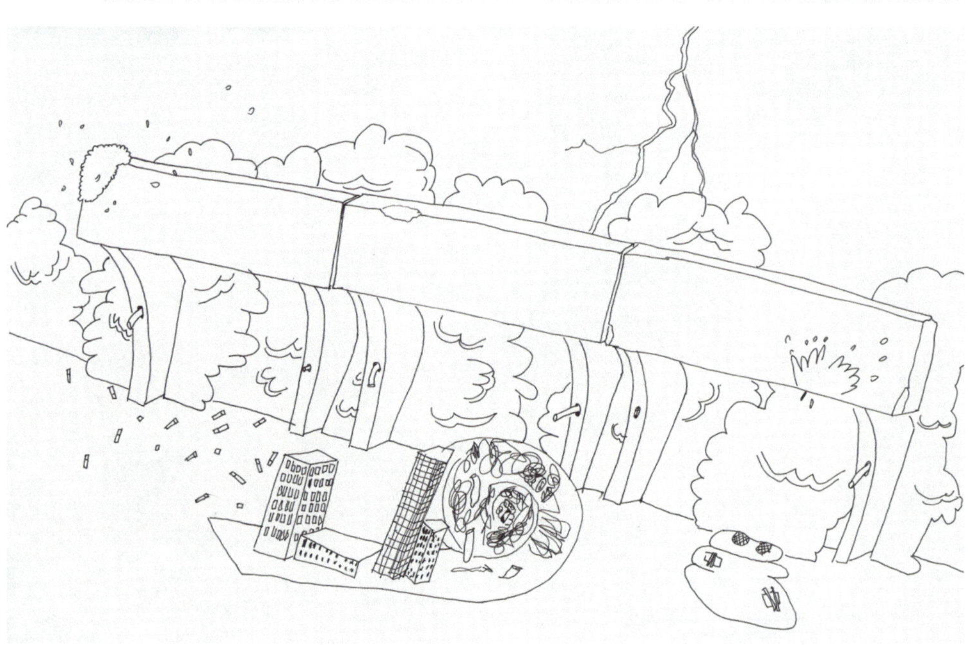

*You Are a
Miserable Lying
Shit and
We Hate You*

Bruce Hainley

'Word.'
(Do hip types—does anyone?—still confirm some comment
about the world by saying 'Word'? Locution-tired or not, it's
what I feel most days about most people, you is the you I was
thinking about as I typed the words, *you are a miserable
lying shit and we hate you*. Word.)

*

I kept most of the jpegs of Ronay's work in a folder labeled
IRAQ. Embedded, I've been collecting other kinds of images for
months, until it (the activity, the specifics of the collecting)
became too much—too ____________. Pix of young American
soldiers, cologned with the satisfaction of their gun-toting,
being fit and becoming men: posing nude in a shower stall;
before shipping out, flexing shirtless in the barracks; over
there, straddling a missile launcher in the desert, turning it into
a monster cock, and later scribbling on the snapshot the
words *Actual Size* with an arrow pointing to their crotch. I find
these photos infinitely poignant. My tears mix with my cum,
looking at them.

*

Ronay's work is all made during wart time. Whether you or he
like(s) it or not. Stacks of CompoundW boxes—ammunition—
in the medicine cabinet. I mean, war time, genital and otherwise. I have nothing more to say about this.

*

Really, Ronay's pieces, a brouhaha, are all made by Kevin
Federline in the basement of Britney's mansion, where, exiled,

he curses as he sands the MDF, over and over. Breeding is
easier. I have nothing more to say about this except fuck it, he
thinks.

*

His violence, representational, conducts itself in broad day-
light, seemingly sunny affects too often misunderstood to be
childlike or toying, instead of bent, sinister. Step on crack-
whore, break your mother's backdoor, slice it into cunty bits,
and bury them beneath the floorboards.

*

In Palermo, 1933, at the Grande Albergo e delle Palme,
Raymond Roussel, high on barbiturates, doting on Soneryl, his
favorite, attacked himself with a razor, but not to off himself:
the bloody parenthetical slits (interstitial, '*moi*' remained
in-between) opened a temporal rift, time's lunette. Out leapt
Öyvind Fahlström. He suggested they play a game. 'I likes
games,' Raymond slurred, lightheaded. An elaborate puzzle of
interrelationships, the this replacing the that—palm fronds
as ball-ticklers; tuning forks in their urethrae, catheter-like, each
pure tone at 440 Hz, chimed for good vibrations (they ((the
same referred to in the phrase 'they say')) call it 'sounding',
my dear); paperweights of leftover Gruyère; underwear as
tam-o'-shanter (fecal pompom)—occupied them into the wee
hours. Employing bizarre self-regulations, intricate rules,
and private grammars, they were not in pursuit of narratives or
systems, while partaking of both but being neither, and when
their gaming stilled into vibrant tableaux it disrupted most,
constructing what they really desired—other worlds bettering,
briefly, this one, change itself, tornadoes of becoming caught
in a highball glass or seeping, patent and fartlike, from the
French kiss of a cat's anus. Their interventions, variables see-
sawing the aesthetic and the political, unnaturally, brought
them, exhilarated, almost exhausted, to the edge of climax,
which they resisted for hours, aid of the Kama Sutra, until,
hung-over, Öyvind popped, slipping into the opening beneath

the umlaut of his first name, a goner. Raymond caught some
of his heavy release in a shot glass and, dipping his Mont-
blanc into it, used it as the invisible ink with which he wrote
his will, his chauffeur doubling as notary. The following day,
after this acrobatic coitus, Roussel OD'd on pills. At least one
biographer reports his valet, Orlando, 'recalled that Roussel
had ejaculated, perhaps during his death throes, like the
hanged man of *Nouvelles Impressions d'Afrique*, who "*pendant
l'ivresse, avant le serrement complet*" (during the intoxication,
before complete constriction) has no need of an aphrodisiac.'
A lawyer for the estate ushered the jism, posthaste, to a
sperm bank in Louisville, Kentucky, where it was frozen until
1976, when, thawed out and turkey-basted, it helped in the
conception of the artist, whose Franco-Swedish heritage has
been rarely noted, like the fact that his birthday coincides,
synchronously, with Fahlström's death date.

*

While the preceding isn't allegory, I could still put things less
allegorically: proposing tableaux for (psychic? somatic?
intellectual?) transformation with mock-ups looking nothing like
mock-ups (i.e. their finish refutes the mock of 'mock-up', which
is not to say, exactly, the mockery, leaving them slyly only
what they are), all the while transmuting the pictorial into the
sculptural (more on this later), Ronay enables OD'ing without death throes, his affects aphrodisiacal, with all the concu-
piscence, conceptual cunnilingus, and cons (linguistic, visual)
available, cum rags included.

*

Hanging men in a landscape; hula hoops hung with condoms;
mushroom penises; conveyor-belt burgers, cocks with bites;
dilated assholes; white shape with turds and bloody toilet
paper; cupcake anal beads, finish line, half-dog-half-little-girl
fucked by patent leather black dildo; two figures behind
fences, diarrhea, sandwiches, cocks; blond-haired, blue-eyed
soldier, sweating (facialed); black torso bumblebee butts,

candles, again with the anal beads (this time, diarrhea-fouled);
muscle man anal leakage, ghostly light-skinned black guy
with ear stretchers; faces, fences, and cummy Kleenexes; cityscape, tongued garbage bags, severed bleeding parts, hives,
Black Power-salute acid blotters and cigarette-shotgun shells.
Call it the *stuff* of the imaginary detonated but not exploding
until it's *in the head*.

*

Forlornness, a peppercorn among the candy whimsy. Becketty
attempts (*I can't go on, I will go on*) to fit this into that, this
cupcake into that ball sac, this limp proboscis into that electri-
cal socket, akin to the mating rituals (drapery of flesh heaved
aside, tiring) of major fatties.

*

Vibrant colors—fir green, ketchup red, urine yellow, 'flesh'
tones (cocoa to tan to pink), licorice, 'interiors' hues (greige,
seashell), fudge brown—along with pristine, precise facture,
operate, like the dewy 'tongues' of carnivorous plants, as lures
or trapdoors into violence represented, implicit and explicit,
a representational violence (hanged men, bit dicks, reamed
assholes) attuned to the violence always already within repre-
sentation. The dilated orifices, diarrhea splatters, severed,
bleeding body parts, and other giggling aftermaths propel the
viewer out of the straightforwardly visual and into unverifia-
bility of the fictive yet without the conclusiveness of linear
storytelling or plot device. If the novelistic is most readily found
outside the novel, the photographic outside the photograph
(brush up on your Barthes if this sounds unfamiliar), Ronay
avails himself of the novelistic and textual in the midst of pur-
suing the tensions and attenuations of word and object. Rather
than confusing or unintentional, the nonnarratives Ronay sets
up are deployed almost as if the objects, a rambunctious array
of recognizable elements, from mushrooms and hula hoops
to hamburgers and Hefty bags, could be used like a vocabulary,
arranged and/or combined to articulate something coherent,

and yet just when what's most desired is for a salving, solving
fable the objects boomerang back into mute objecthood, leaving all things contingent, 'their splendor', as Foucault intoned
while harnessed and gangbanged in a dank backroom, 'is
not that deployed by our eyes but that defined by sequential
elements of syntax'. It's not as if anyone couldn't make 'sense'
of Ronay's tableaux, but the hallucinogenic vividness of his
objects' recognizability and hue demand, somewhat paradoxi-
cally, questioning why so many wish to resist nonknowledge
or nonsense, even abstraction. Availing himself of a clarity and,
despite all the depicted messes and soilings, a spic-and-span
technique associated with Surrealism (Ronay's drooping condoms drop hits and hints of Dalì, and, like his sagging clocks,
they're ways of keeping time) and how dreams are recalled,
when they are recalled, Ronay draws us into his dimensionality
only to strand us comically back in the world—whose bar-
barism is suddenly, as a consequence of having escaped as figures moving, momentarily, within and around his looking-glass,
acid environments, much too close and point-blank.

*

All the while, it's fun to make something look like something
else. It is lovely to notice something looking like what it's not.

*

This part is called hygiene and feces—I mean, fences. Hygiene
requires metaphorical fencing, the clean kept from the dirty,
the dirty kept from the clean. Of course, dirt in the bathroom
is just fertile ground for gardening in the backyard.

*

Lightning flashes, creating a bustle in the greenery behind
what looks like 'cement' support structure for a highway; holes
extruding severed limbs or dripping with sanguine stool punc-
tuate the base of the cement arches. Dwarfed below (or merely
'faraway', the change in scale a perspective of distance),
three 'buildings' and a 'skyscraper' rest on top of the grooved

red 'tongue' of a party blowout, murky green plastic bags
wedged in the coils of its unfurled tip. To the right of the cityscape, a three-tiered Caucasian 'pink' ('white'?) tuffet, part-
penis, part-breast, party protrusion, sprouts sparse, stiff black
pubic hairs; clean gauze bandages cover what might be a
chancre. A swarm of wingless bees festers at the upper left
corner of the cement structure, while scattered on the same
plane as the cityscape are shotgun shells passing themselves
off as chubby cigarette butts and acid blotters with a Black
Power fist logo. Scale shifts dramatically, everything at once
too big and too small for what it resembles and with what
it's in proximity, deranging any simple vantage.

*

Unusually, in *To Possess It, One Must Walk Through It At
Night*, Ronay calls attention to facture: bumps and paint scuffs
connote the drag and wear of time as much as the constructed
artifice of the endeavor. Mimesis and verisimilitude remain
core issues, what such terms still could mean in a world and
moment contrived by the virtual and the clone. Employing
different styles of rendering—while the shrubbery recalls
E. C. Segar's Popeye backgrounds (Wimpie, with his economy
of hamburgers, loiters around many of Ronay's affairs) as
well as John Wesley's winsome domains and the stubbled
tuffet operates like something out of Woody Allen's *Sleeper*,
the plastic bags and acid blotters hone in, verisimilarly, to
what might be considered the actual or possible—Ronay works
through the logic and violence of how the world comes to
resemble how it's represented. The pieces brought together
for *Goin' Down, Down, Down* deploy finish lines, fences,
hedgerow bushes, and even more unlikely delimiters (sheets,
anal beads) of the living from the dead, of the inside from
the out, of the private from the public. His nocturnal emission,
looking as much like what it depicts as what it isn't depicting,
occurs diurnally, as Ronay puts mimesis through its paces,
commanding it to convey what isn't seen to be present but is.
Gunshots, acid trips, we're taking hits—and just because

aesthetic and metaphorical doesn't mean without consequence.
Everything's just so, until it craps out, and we're wallowing
in our own shit—psychic and actual. At a time when borders
are patrolled and contested, when things are done 'over there'
so as not to occur 'at home'—*home*, a word which should
leave many more at a loss—it's not so clear or it's entirely too
clear that orientation can't be habitually accomplished,
secured. The compass keeps breaking as we're smuggled ille-
gally, along and across borders between the real and what
comes to stand-in for it as if, codependent, we're no longer
able to tell on which side of the border anyone remains.
Word.

*

And, verily, is all of it true?
Um, did you read the title? There are more ways to truth than
by the front door, and his is, among other things, a backdoor
aesthetic to say the least. The very least.

*

Walked through at night, most things disappear in the dark.

*

Enough of that shit.
If things have gotten stuck in the bilge of the highfalutin,
'scuse me while I fart instead of kissing the sky. Cutting one
reminds me to mention the gassy traditions of high art in the
most recent centuries, Piero Manzoni's canned desublimation
not the half of it. Now, some of you—yeah, you—might be
asking, Well, Bruce, fuck him, who's he? I'm the chief curator
of the first ever International Fart Biennial. When someone
takes an impressive dump, our employees are encouraged to
think of it as upgrading their Thetan level. In the early after-
noon, our staff meetings occur in offices become postprandial
Dutch ovens.
    My idea files include notes on key—not as much first
and second as number one and number two—moments.

Note #1: In Warhol's great flick, *Screen Test #2*, Ronald Tavel, scintillating off-screen presence, feeds Mario Montez lines. She mimes and mopes, she twirls, both Esmerelda and Quasimodo. In one divine sequence, Tavel demands she repeat the word, diarrhea, in various accents and with numerous intensities, insisting she savor it, like a caramel, and noting her embouchure.

Note #2: Too often taken to be stern Michael Snow, after the staunch revolutions of La Région Centrale, made *'Rameau's Nephew' by Diderot (Thanx to Dennis Young) by Wilma Schoen*. In this study of sound, synched and unsynched, and image, the opening credits are read by a stutterer forced to keep up with the scrolling cast titles. There's a fart sequence, in which everyone speaks in a backward language, and, at the most excruciating moment in this 266-minute opus, long past a convenient pause, a punning 'pee break', with nudes, a man and a woman, each finding relief by pissing into resonant, empty tin tubs. Of course, 'Wilma Schoen' herself, already in the film's title, embodies the first of many anagrams, puns, turns and twists of language depicted, since 'Wilma Schoen' is 'Michael Snow' spelled anagrammatically.

Note #3: Many of Steven Parrino's prepossessing paintings look like butt holes, sometimes like Bridget Rileys butt-holed.

I have oodles of other notes.

Ronay's oeuvre, a veritable alimentary canal of goodies, things put in the mouth or anus and finding their way out of other orifices—dental dammings, rectal jammings; fistings, feedings and dumpings; all kinds of eructation, fumigations, dumplings—participates in this pungent vein. He puts anality in the driver's seat, as it were, for a homosexual cruise not dependent on the dutifully productive family values of repro-ductivity but on pleasure. If you don't believe me, and why should you, folks, here's a little Guy Hocquenghem to bring this, almost, to the end:

All homosexuality is concerned with anal eroticism, whatever the differentiations and perverse re-territorialisations

*to which the Oedipus complex subsequently subjects it. The
anus is not a substitute for the vagina: women have one
as well as men. The phallus's signifying-discerning function is
established at the very same moment that the anus-organ
breaks away from its imposed privatization, in order to take part
in the desire race. To reinvest the anus collectively and libidi-
nally would involve a proportional weakening of the great phallic
signifier, which dominates us constantly both in the small-
scale hierarchies of the family and in the great social hierarchies. The least acceptable desiring operation (precisely
because it is the most desublimating one) is that which is
directed at the anus.*

And, one might say, *by* it. (Whenever I use the word,
desublimating, SpellCheck wants to replace it with *desali-
nating*.) Honorary faggot, Ronay puts us on both sides of the
finish line of the desire race. His nonsites of waste rim sites
of pleasure, roam, becoming them, sounding them. As one of
George Kuchar's videos puts it, *Chili Line Stops Here*, and
with his fulfilling Dinty Moore aesthetic, Kuchar should know.
Johnny Quicksteps, it keeps chugging along, seeping here
that is everywhere.

Interview
with
Matthew
Ronay

Michael Glover

It is a blazing, high summer's day in North London, almost hot
enough to steam-iron you to the pavement, and Matthew
Ronay, a young man from Kentucky (though he now lives and
works in New York) is in a hurry. The plane came via Green-
land, and it arrived two hours behind schedule. Next day he is
off to Istanbul. But today it's London, and we're alive in the
important moment of the catalogue interview.

He accepts a succulent red cherry from the bowl on
the meeting room's round table, then goes out of doors to
smoke a quick cigarette. When he returns, just moments later,
he whips out his laptop, very small and very slender, and
shows me some of the latest work, the work he's been making
for his show here, his first major London outing.

There will be three large new pieces, two of which are
already made. They are tableaux-like scenes. The rest of
his exhibition will consist of groups of works which have been
exhibited in Marc Foxx's Los Angeles gallery and at Vacio 9
in Madrid. This is a young man much in demand, both for
group and solo shows.

As usual, the works are very bright and emphatic, and
they consist of strange concatenations of objects, things
fused together that might only get joined up in dreams, or in
bizarre waking reveries. That doesn't mean there's anything
otherworldly about the atmosphere of these pieces. They are
very much rooted in the here and now of contemporary
culture and politics.

I watch him as he shifts, quickly, from image to image.
There's nothing virtual or conceptual here, I notice. These
big and often extravagantly, and even self-delightingly, trans-
gressive objects work together to form what often look a

little like theatre sets. They're that large, that imposing. The primary colours slam against our eyes, like fists.

Everything Matthew Ronay does he seems to do with a quick, slightly nervy, whippet-like eagerness, as though there is no time to be lost. When I begin to speak to him, to question him about his life and his work, he looks back at me very intently, very searchingly. His hair is close-cropped, his brown eyes cautiously wary.

I talk to him about the exhibition at the Astrup Fearnley Museum of Modern Art in Oslo, in the autumn of last year, where I first saw his work. Called *Uncertain States of America*, it showcased the work of an entire generation of younger American artists: painters, video-makers, installation artists, sculptors. I tell him how disappointed I had been by the two-dimensional work in the show, how weak and derivative it seemed to be for the most part: tired images of images culled from popular culture. The real energy came when you turned into the spaces devoted to sculpture, to the work of Taft Green and Cristina Lei Rodriguez, and a third young sculptor called Matthew Ronay.

What was it about all this three-dimensional work which pleased me so much? I explain that for me there seemed to be a renewed confidence in the idea of object-making, a confidence – or perhaps even a will – which seemed to have been absent for almost a couple of decades. But is an object-maker necessarily a sculptor? I ask him. Did he recognise what he was doing in my terms of reference?

No, not exactly. Matthew seemed to be coming from somewhere else altogether, some quasi-mystical otherwhere, I noticed when he began to explain his own terms of reference. In fact, this was to become a fairly familiar pattern in the course of our conversation. I would try to propose – or perhaps even to impose, because that is the way of critics – a certain way of thinking upon him, but when he came to reply, it became evident that our languages, and perhaps even our ways of seeing, were some distance apart from each other, that he had deftly managed to slither out from under, and had

popped up somewhere slightly different. Yet that is all in the
nature of interesting conversations. The interlocutors, by inter-
rogating each other repeatedly, and in an atmosphere of
amiability and mutual goodwill, eventually find fruitful ground
on which to stand and set out their respective positions.

Sculptures? What Matthew wanted to explain to me was
the way the objects he made came into being, and perhaps
how they came to be what they were. He begins in drawing,
he tells me, which he does at all times, sometimes during
the night. He does many, many drawings. Some of them are
doodles, and some of them are more finished pieces. Within
these drawings, he occasionally finds a possibility of something
– it may just be a line which has pleased him.

Then, at some point, these drawings or fragments of
drawings get fused with other drawings.

'The drawings can take anything from five seconds to a
minute 30 seconds,' Matthew tells me. 'Then they go up on
the wall. They get edited together. I make an amalgam. At that
point I feel the whole thing has become authored.' He muses
for a moment, wondering about the possibility of a second
cherry. They are very good, I am discovering, especially in
such heat. 'This business of what to call oneself is a difficult
one, you know. I really see myself as an antenna, drawing in
or receiving messages...'

Which is, as it happens, exactly what the poet Ezra
Pound once said: *artists are the antennae of the race*.

And these strange fusions, once received, subsequently
become realised – in fact, almost exactly transcribed, though
some modification is always likely to occur during the making
process – as three-dimensional objects.

Matthew Ronay does all this intensive making work
entirely unaided at the studio he shares with other artists in the
New York borough of Queens. He really feels, he confides,
that he ought by now to be considering the possibility of hiring
some studio assistants to help him with the fabrication of
the work, but he also sighs at the thought of the difficulties
involved in doing so. Why sigh though? Because all these

pieces need to remain entirely his, from beginning to end. And
how could he possibly remain in full control if he handed over
even some part of the task to an alien hand?

'It is an impractical way to work, I know. But being soli-
tary is also useful. I have a vast abyss of time to create
thoughts about meaning. You can get something really rich out
of nothing, you know.'

And the images Matthew Ronay creates are, to many,
transcriptions of *nothing* kind of things, the kind of objects
which society overlooks and discards, which are jettisoned,
despised and robbed of all meaning: a hamburger, or a hamburger wrapper, on the street; a useless blob of fat; garbage
bags; a used Kleenex; batteries.

'I like things of the people,' he tells me, 'things that are
overlooked. I'm not fighting for their rights, but they do have
potential.'

So, in part, are these strange amalgamations of things
'dream objects' of a kind? These are two of the words I had
jotted down in my notebook when I first saw his work at that
show in Oslo last year. I propose this tentatively now, how-
ever, because I know that such a term could lead, almost as
surely as night follows day, to the introduction of the word
surrealism, and I already know that Matthew dislikes the word
surrealism because it is a lazy, catch-all kind of a term which
seems to turn one into a throwback to something rather tired
and long gone. So he has toyed with the term 'hyper-realism',
but rejected that too because it already defines a movement,
and that's not something with which he would want to be
associated. So we lay aside the issue of pigeon-holing and talk
about other matters.

About the objects themselves, what they are made from,
and how they are treated. The surfaces are often brilliantly
colourful and smooth, even highly wrought – like some child's
toy. And yet the subject matter, though it may seem to begin
in various elements we tend to associate with child-appeal –
warmth, brightness, smooth rondure – never ends in that. In
fact, it seems almost violently opposed to it, and as if that

opposition is willed. What begins in calmness and innocence quickly ends in innocence's opposite: violence and guilt. So before our eyes we have strange combinations of: the cooked and the raw, the sacred and the profane, the sweet and the sour, odourlessness and ordure.

And just as the objects he chooses to depict are relatively poor, despised and neglected things in our world of disposable riches, so the materials he tends to use – MDF, for example – are relatively lowly materials.

This fascination with things, things, things, the joining of one thing to another – a condom to a hula hoop, for example – inclines one to believe that Matthew Ronay's first point of reference must be the way in which images of popular culture have been appropriated in American art since at least Warhol onwards. But he insists that the truth is quite otherwise.

'I believe that the biggest influence on my work has been reading, and that is something I never did in a big way till I was at high school. Some of the books which have had the greatest influence on me have been French – the post-war nouveaux romans of such authors as Alain Robbe-Grillet, Raymond Queneau, and others...'

'And what did these writers give you that you could use in your work?'

He carefully explains to me that they pared everything back to some kind of obsessively scrupulous description of the object. 'They elevated the object to such a height that it somehow hands over all the responsibility to the viewer. Yes, this is hyper-visual writing! Or think of Georges Perec's *Life, A User's Manual*. It is such impractical writing, you might say. In order to read the book, you have to participate, fully, with the author. It is a crazy, generous, open-ended, magical thing. To read it you virtually have to write it...

'Borges wrote a famous story, a comic masterpiece, on exactly that theme – the triumphant re-enactment of the writing of *Don Quixote*.'

Matthew storms on, warming to his theme. 'Everything pivots on needing to ask the viewer to give themselves up to creating their own interpretation of what has been written. And, yes, as with the Borges, in order to read it, you virtually have to write it.'

And it is rather similar in the bizarre world of the object-making of Matthew Ronay. This is a world of such willed, alarming and often gracefully graceless serendipity – one in which sex copulates in the foam with death, in which corn stalks mingle with blood – that without throwing yourself in headlong, you will get precisely nowhere, or you will forever be pressing your nose at the sweetshop window, greedily looking inward.

'May I read you a quotation from a film called *Videodrome* by David Cronenberg?' Matthew asks me.

'Of course.'

He pulls out a slim notebook – as he does on other occasions during this interview. It is evidently one of his most faithful friends.

'What I'm going to read to you is an interview, between James Woods and a woman, about an addictive TV show on violence. She speaks first.

'*"But don't you feel that such shows contribute to a social climate of sexual violence and malaise? And do you care?"*

'*"Certainly I care ... I care enough to give my viewers a harmless outlet for their fantasies and their frustrations, and as far as I am concerned, that is a socially positive act."*'

Matthew puts his notebook away. 'When I heard that in the movie, I thought it was really great. And I think it relates to my work.'

'And would you say that your art is likely to alienate the viewer in any way? After all, it can be very alarming, on a number of levels.'

'On the contrary. I feel, if anything, that it has a kind of false generosity.'

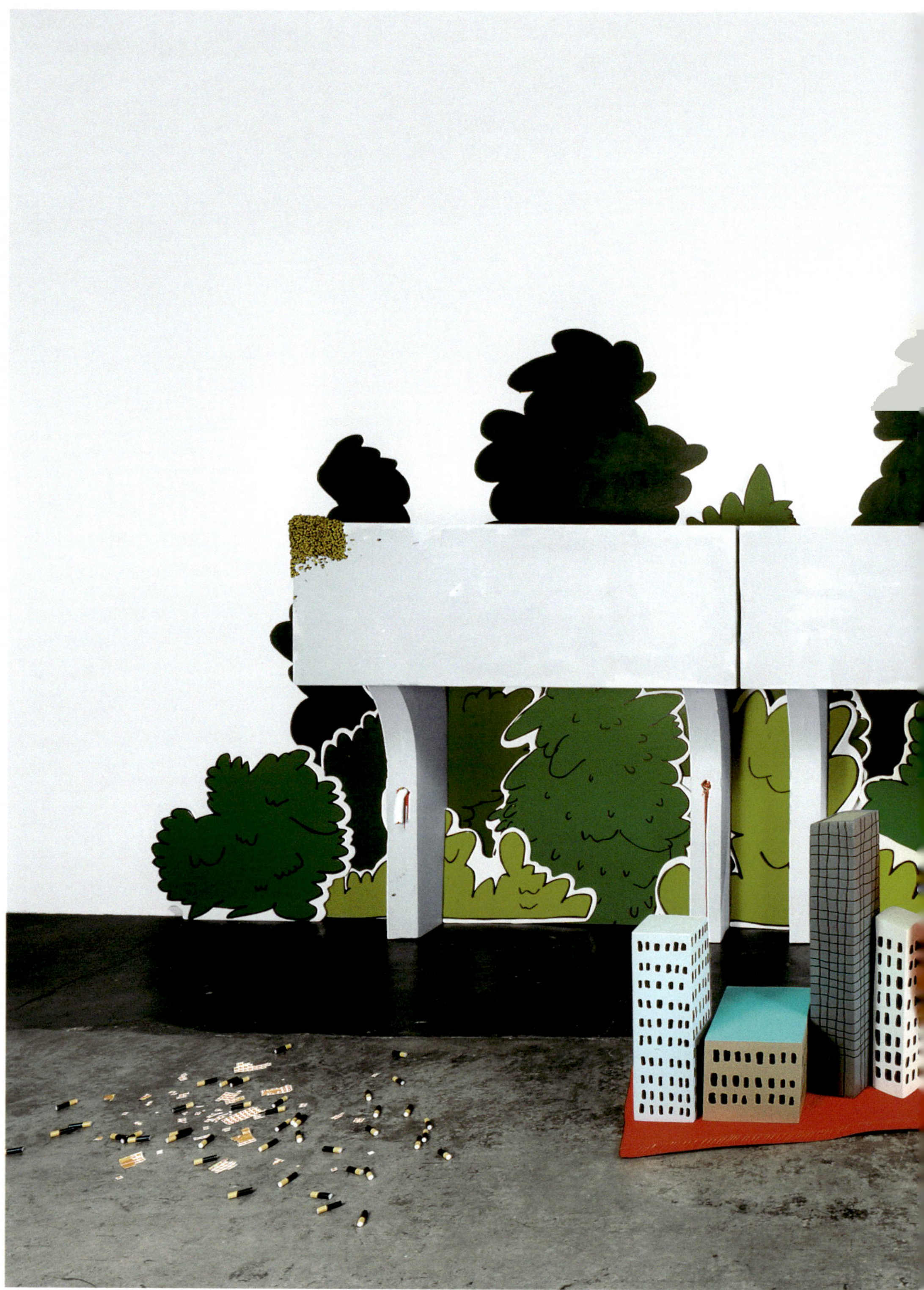

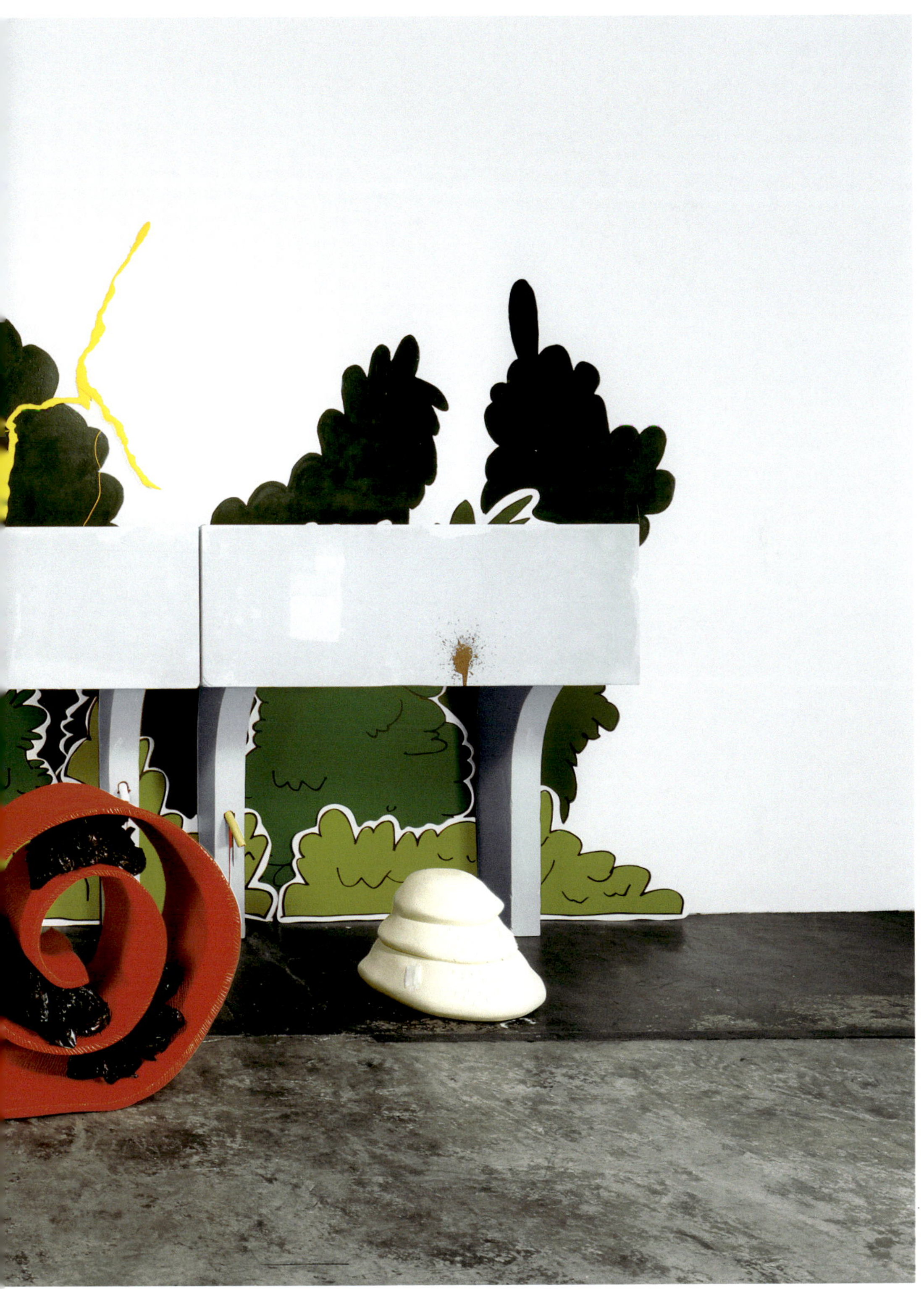

55   *To Possess It, One Must Walk Through It At Night*, 2006

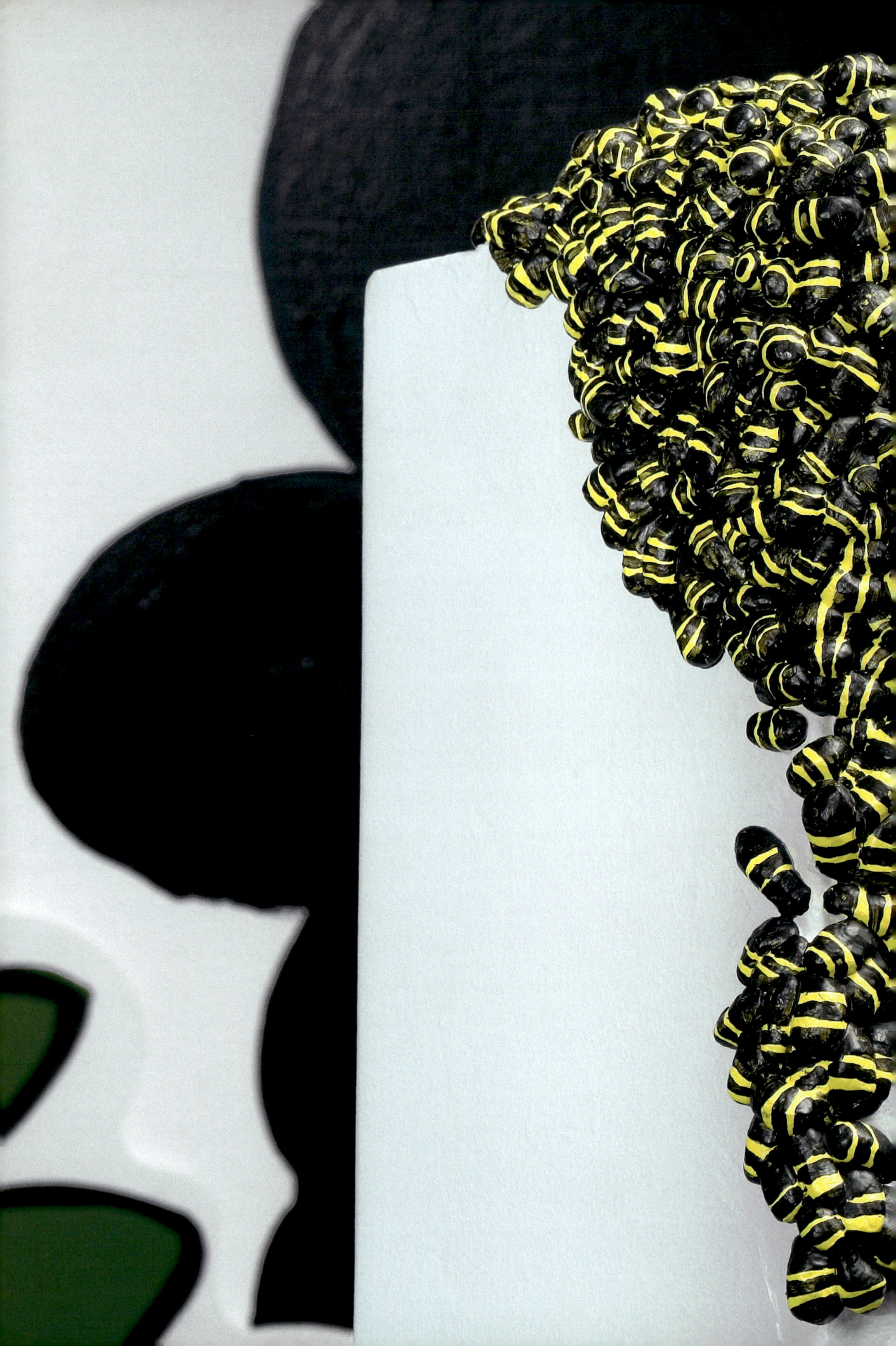

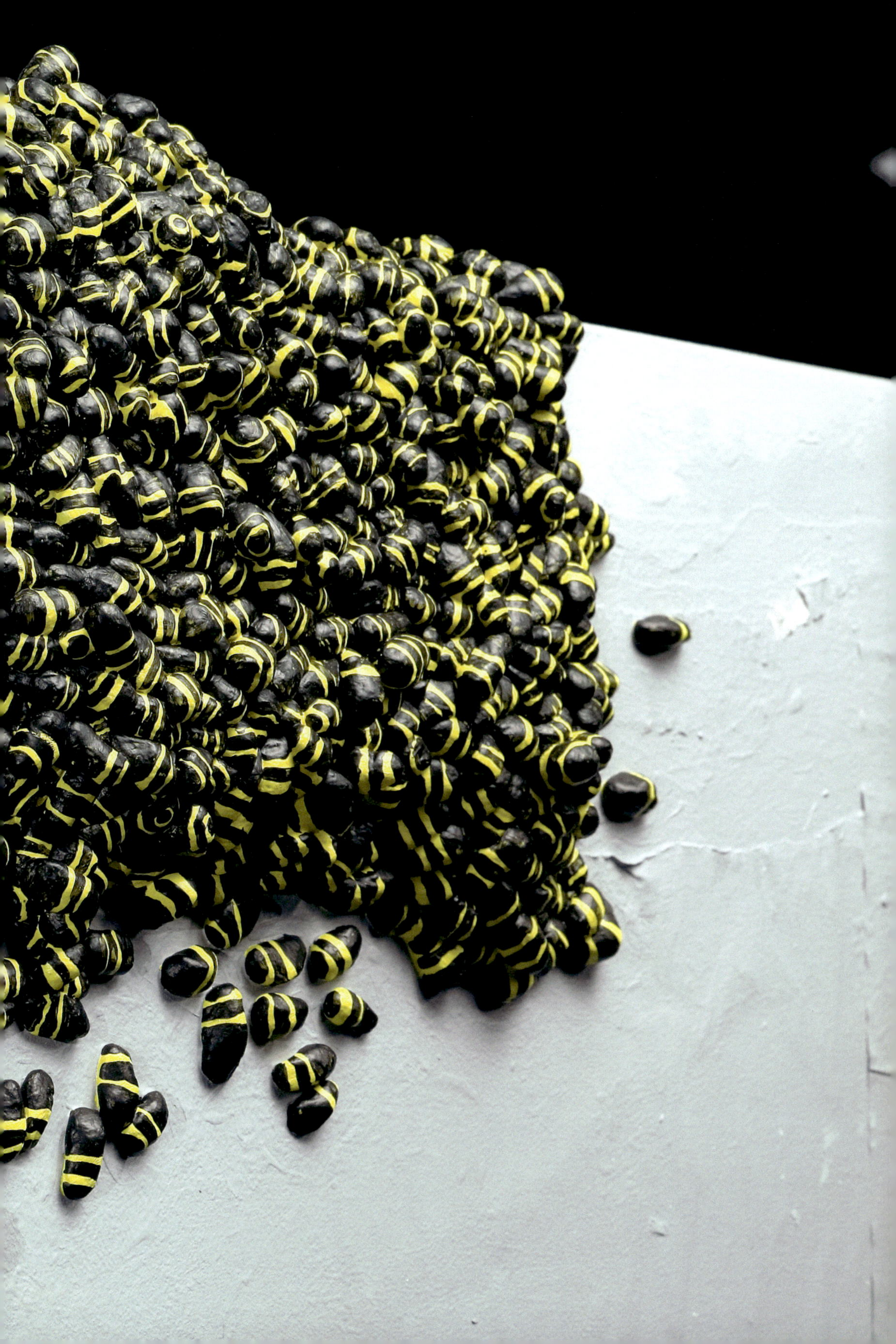

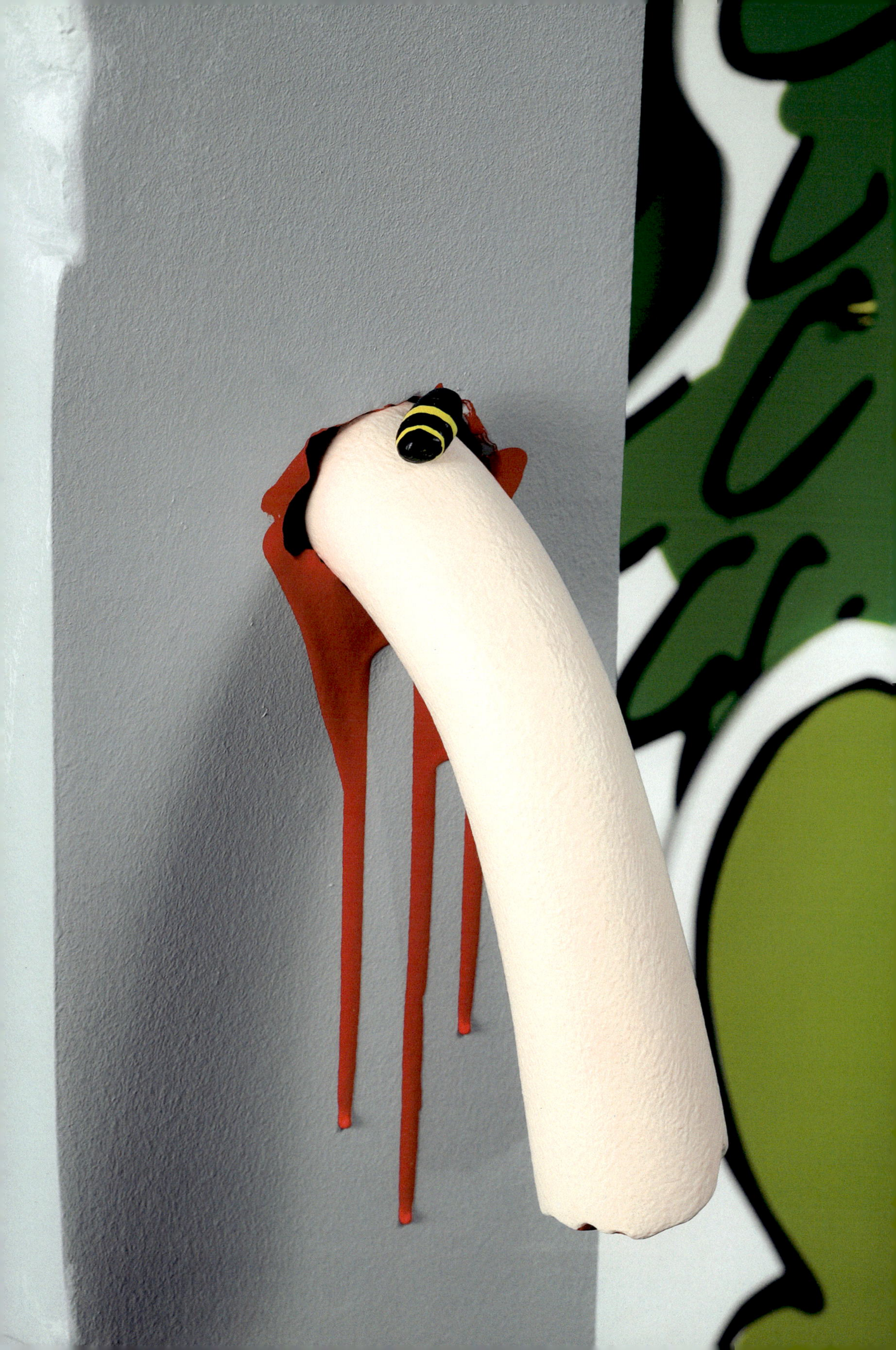

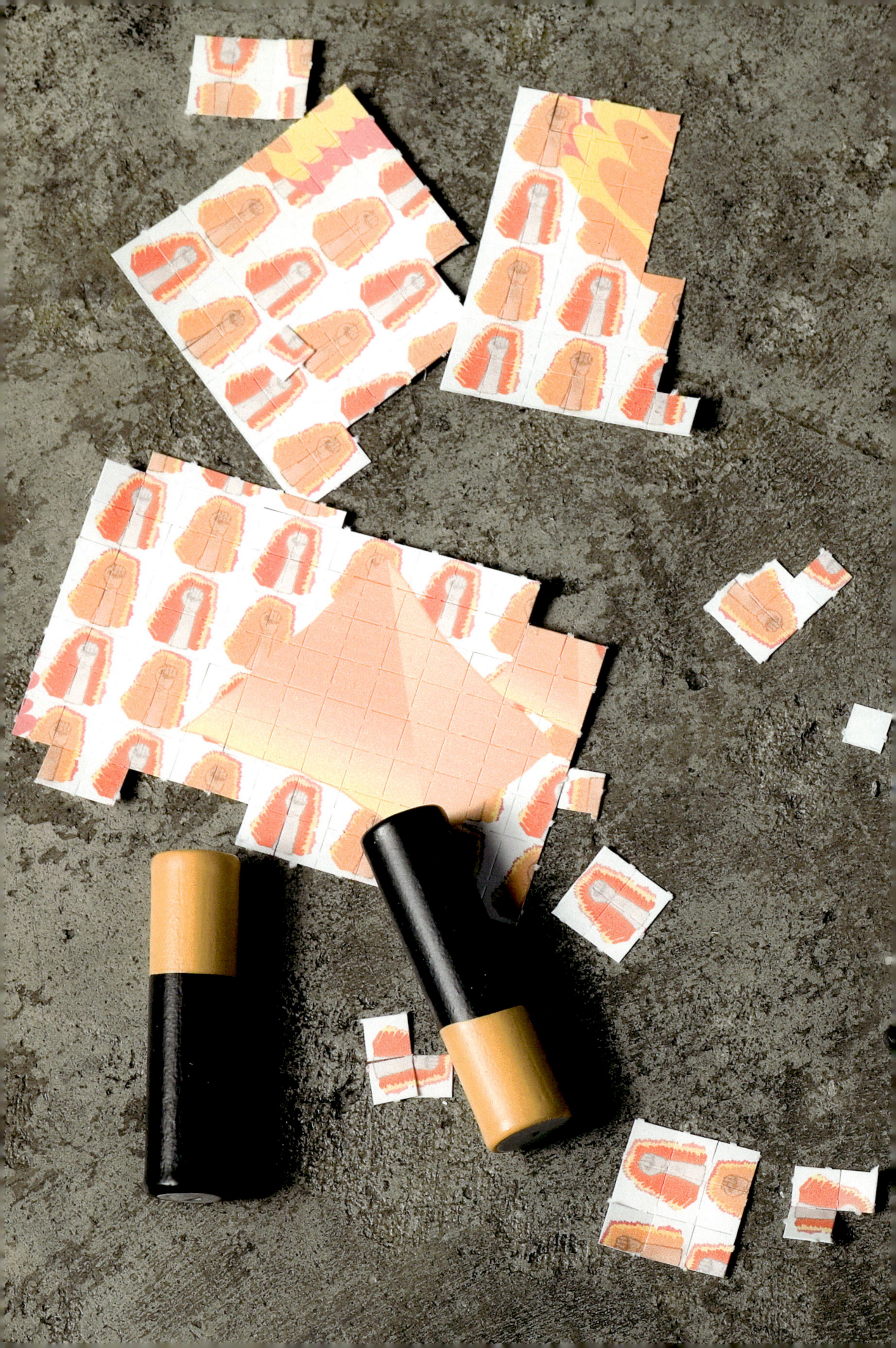

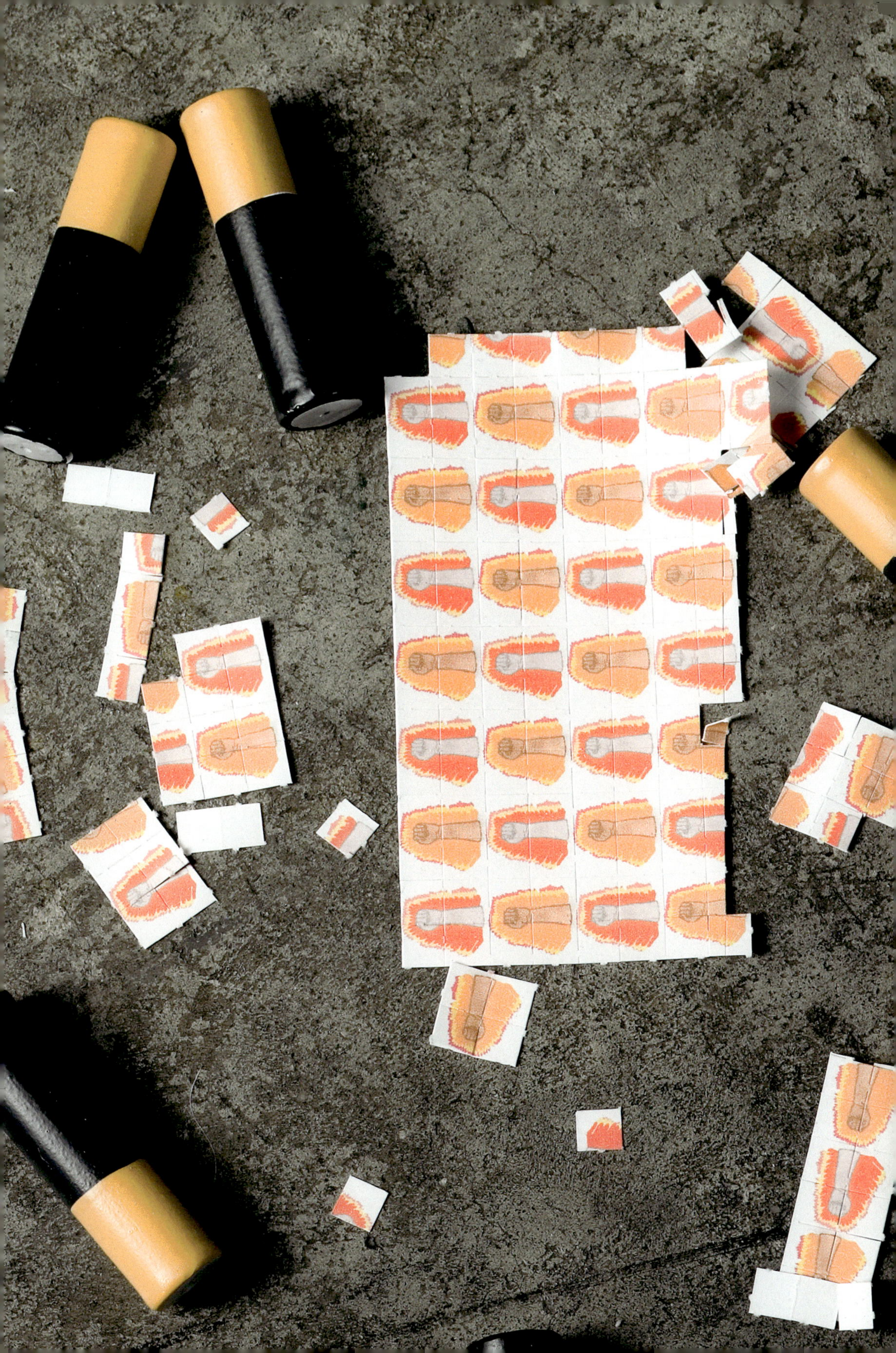

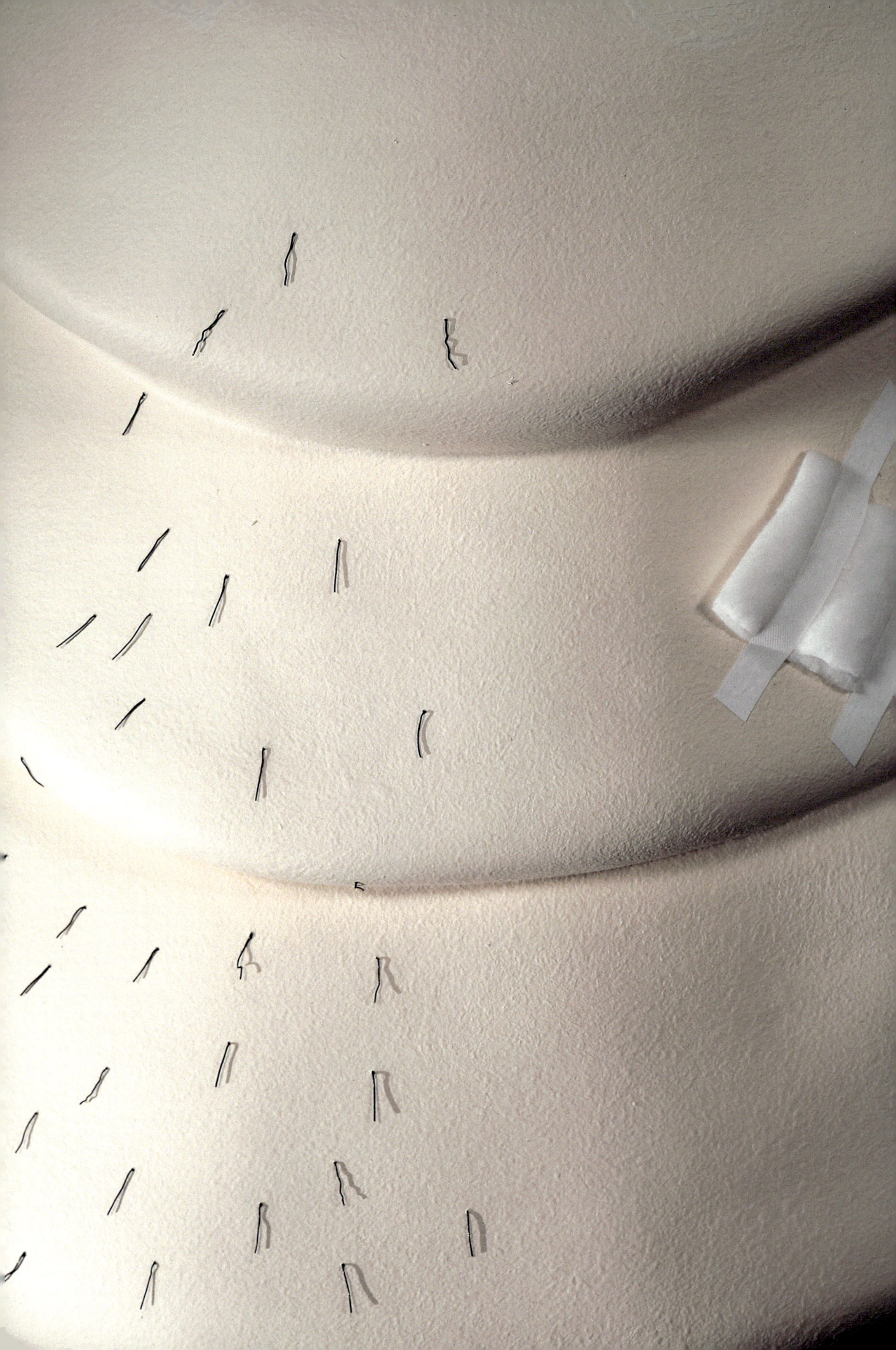

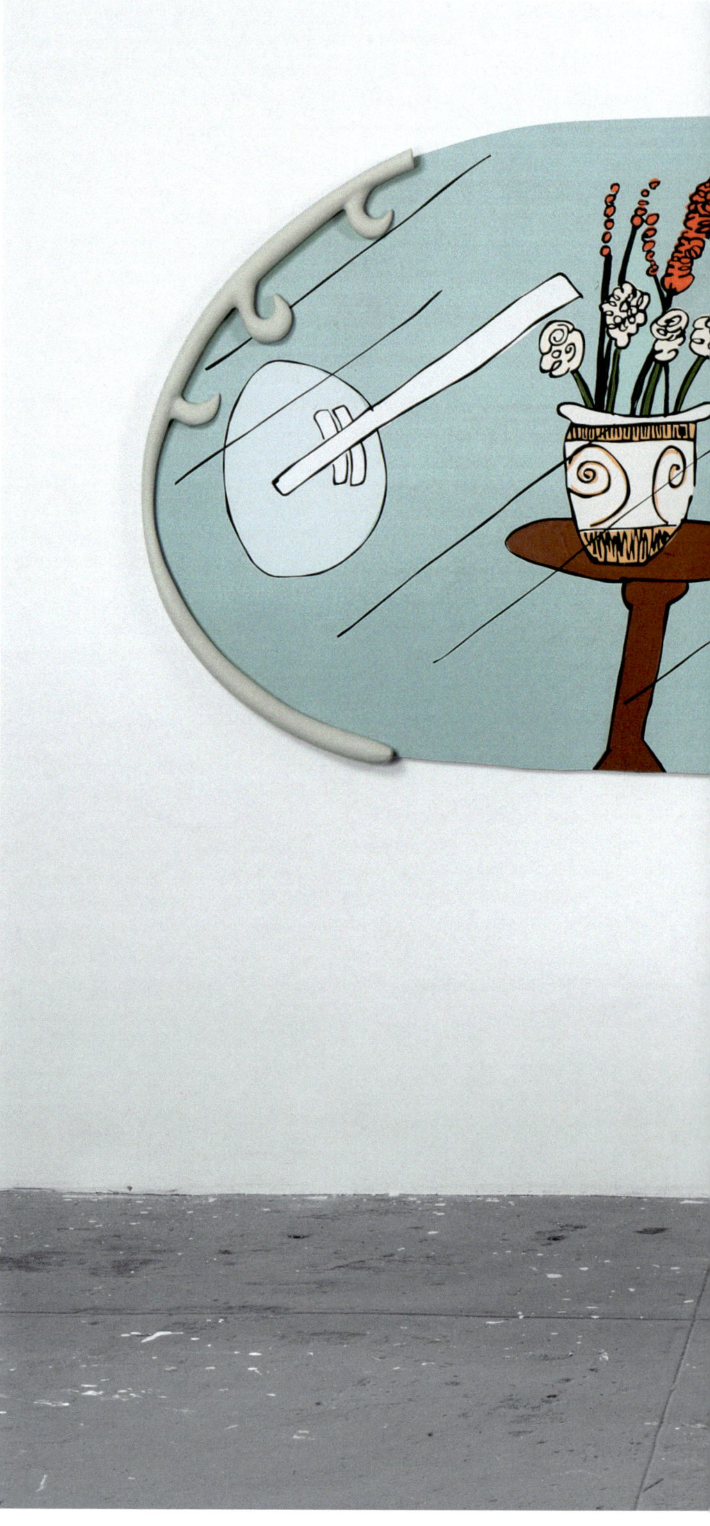

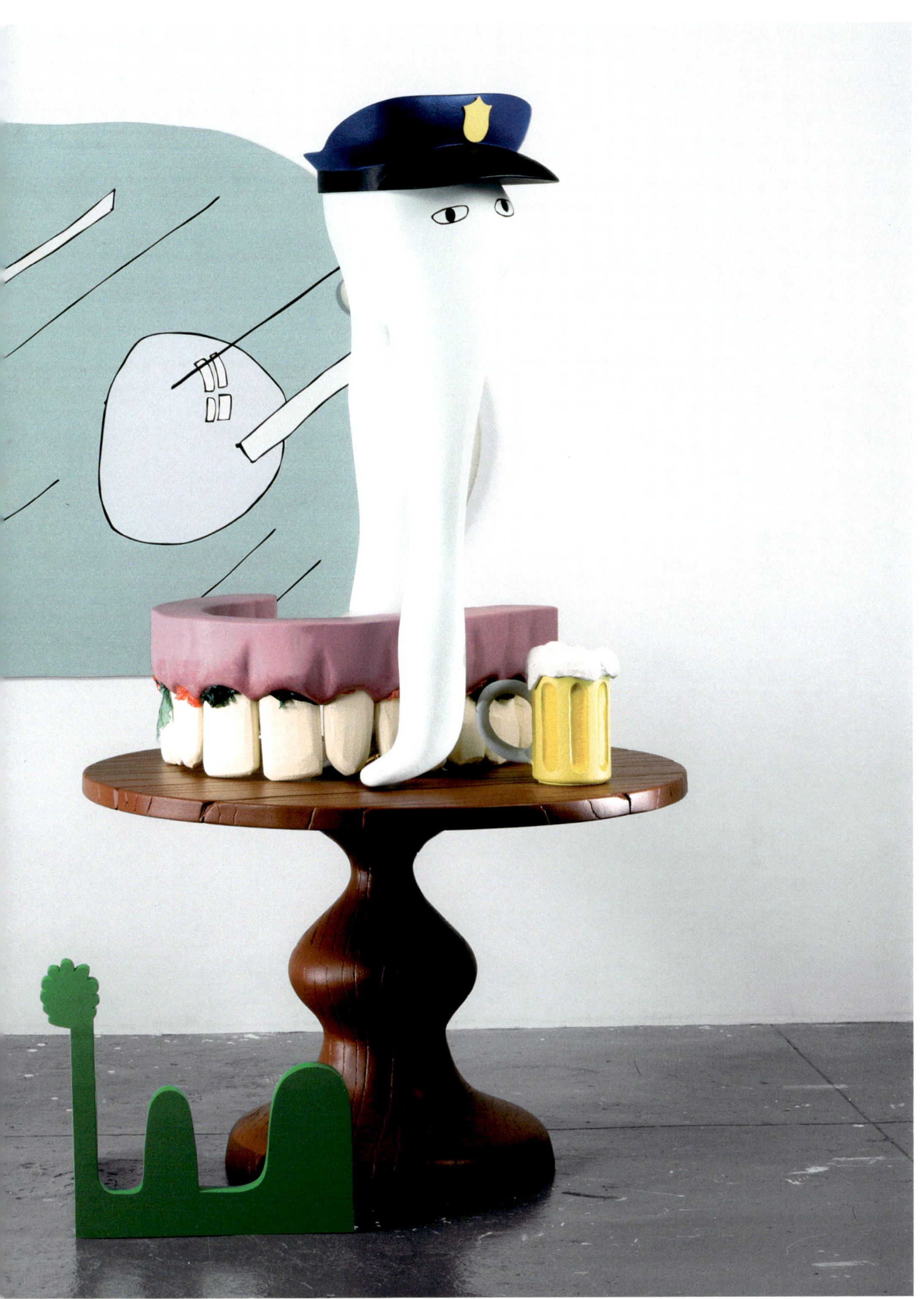

65   *Officer, Officer, Officer, Officer!*, 2006

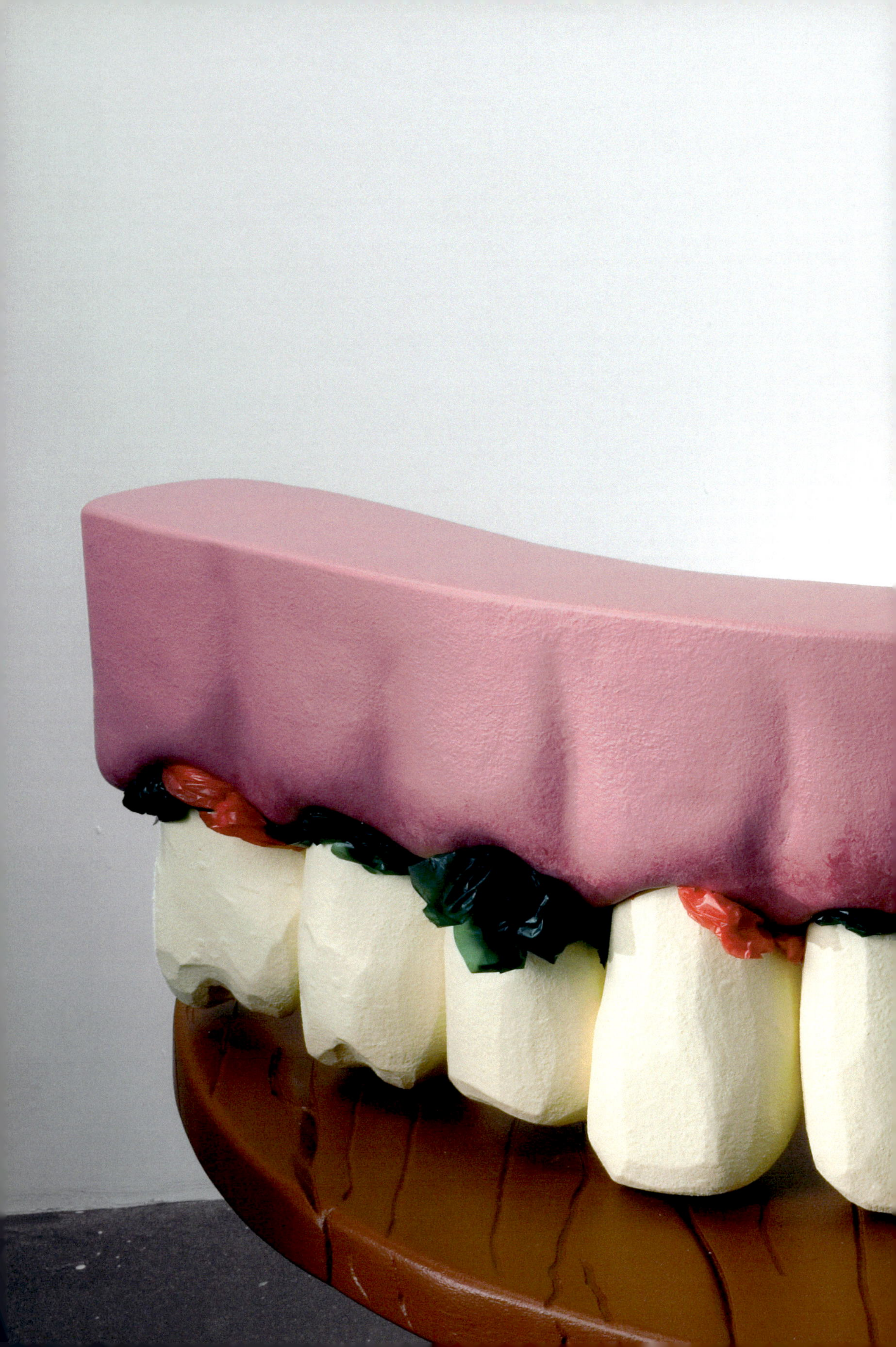

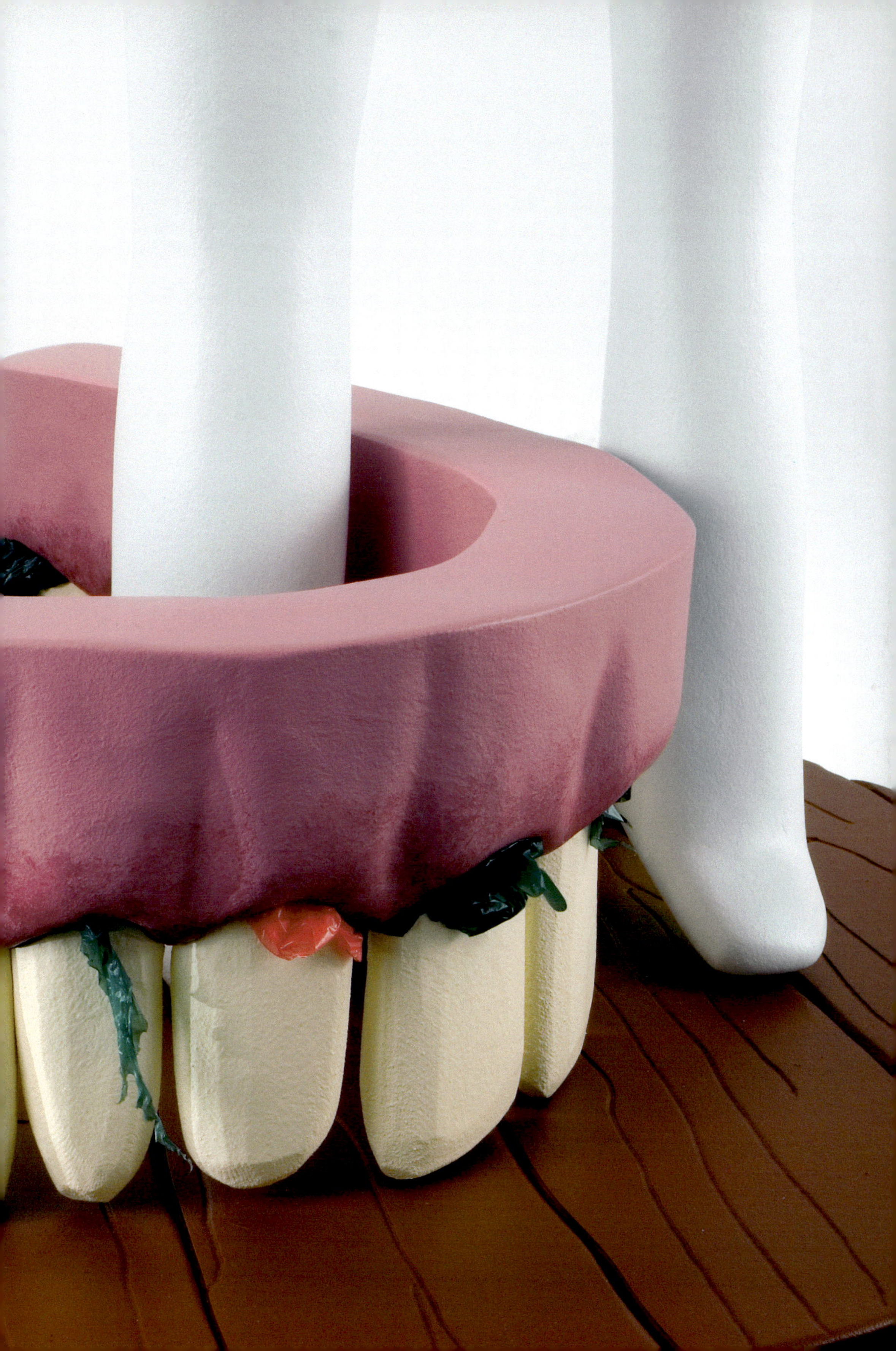

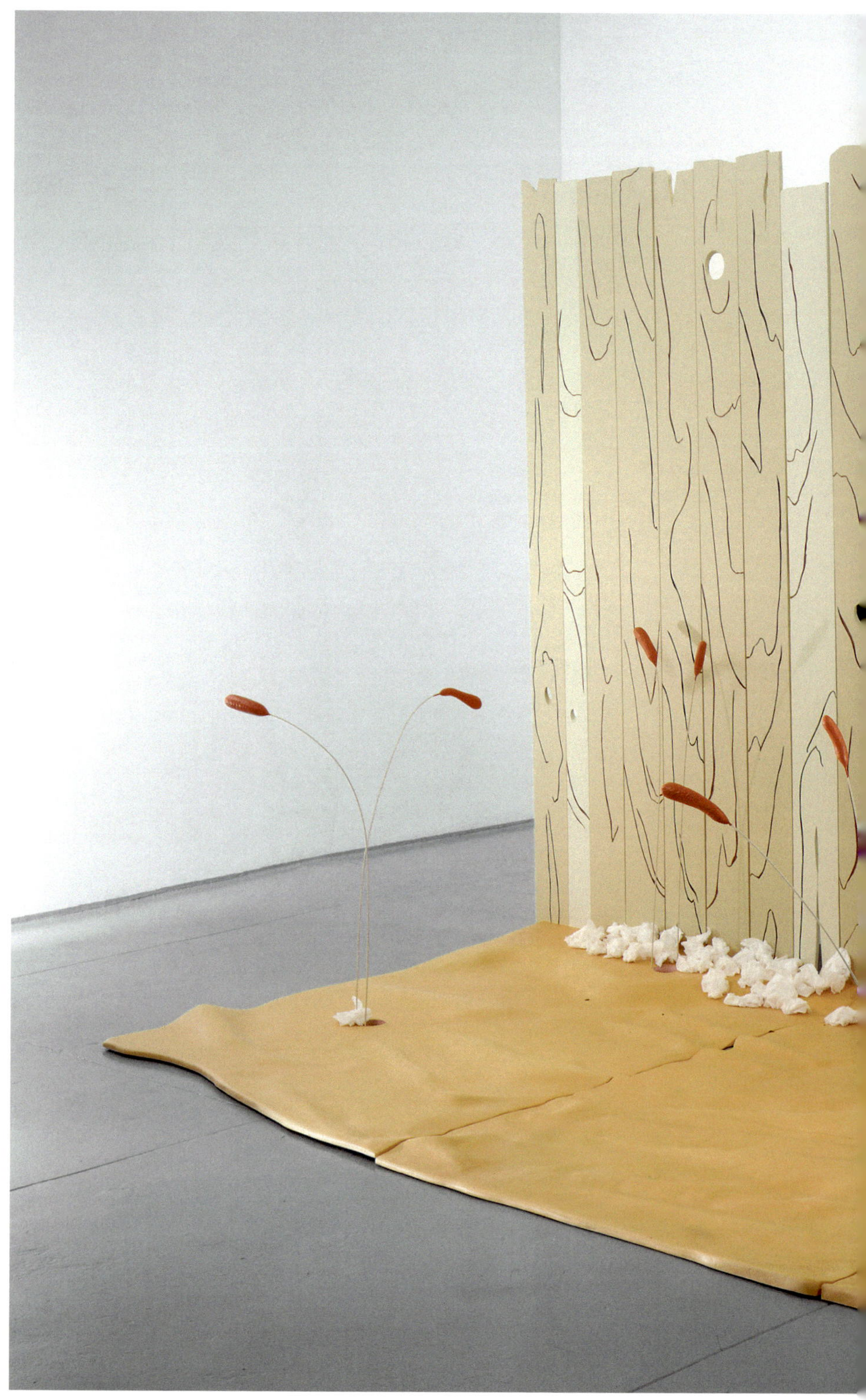

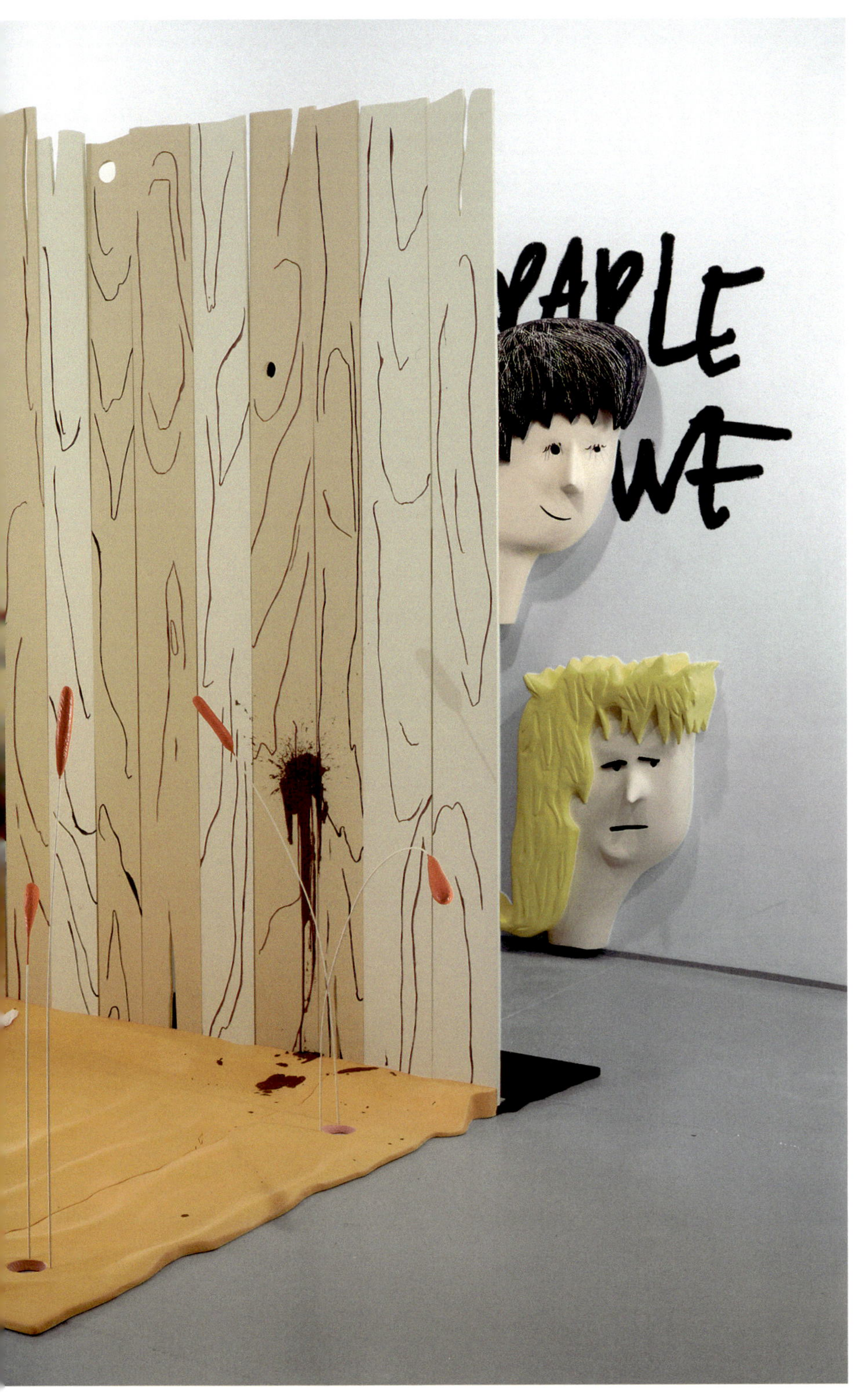

    Don't Stop…Don't Stop the Feelin', 2006

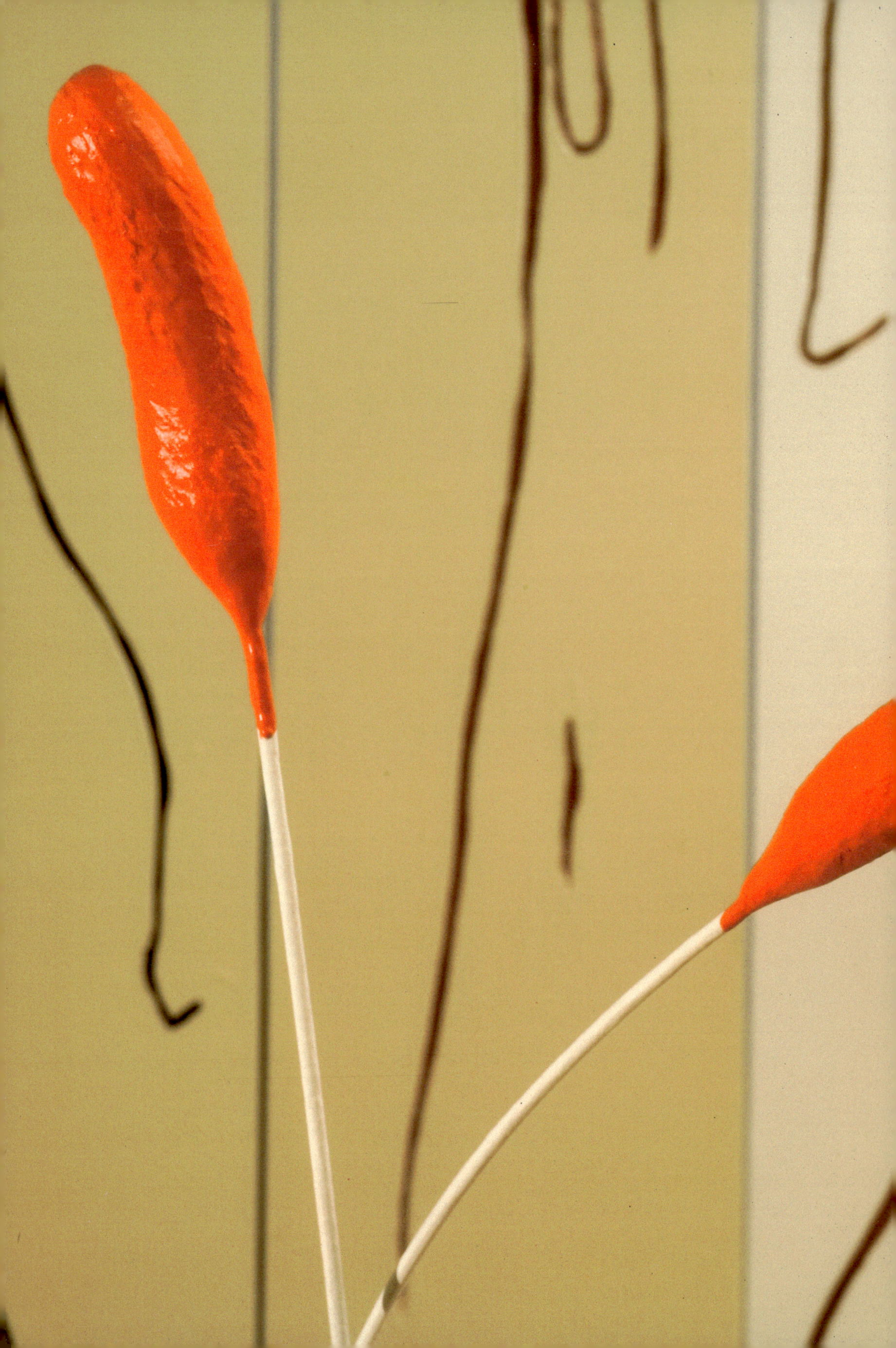

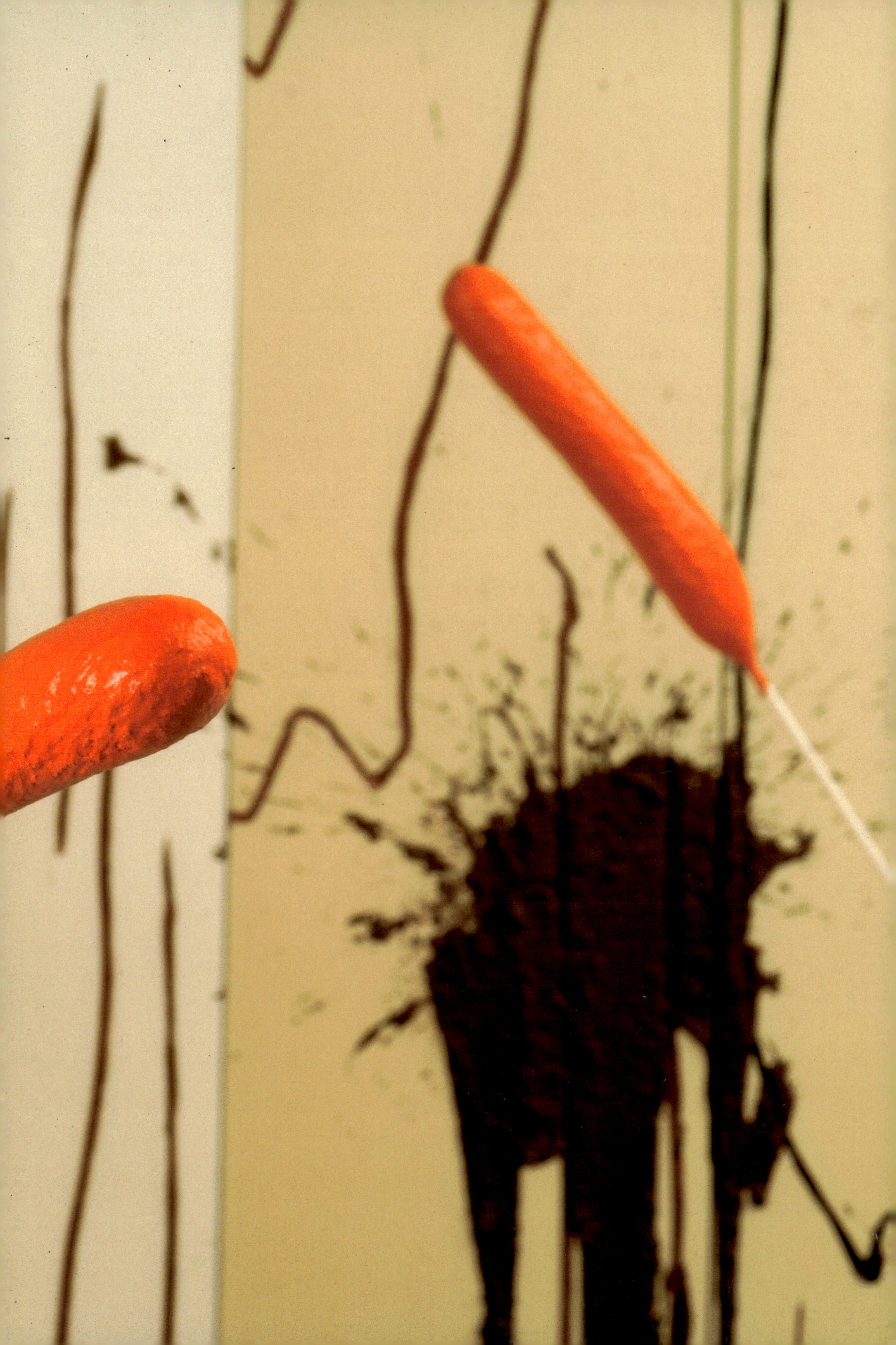

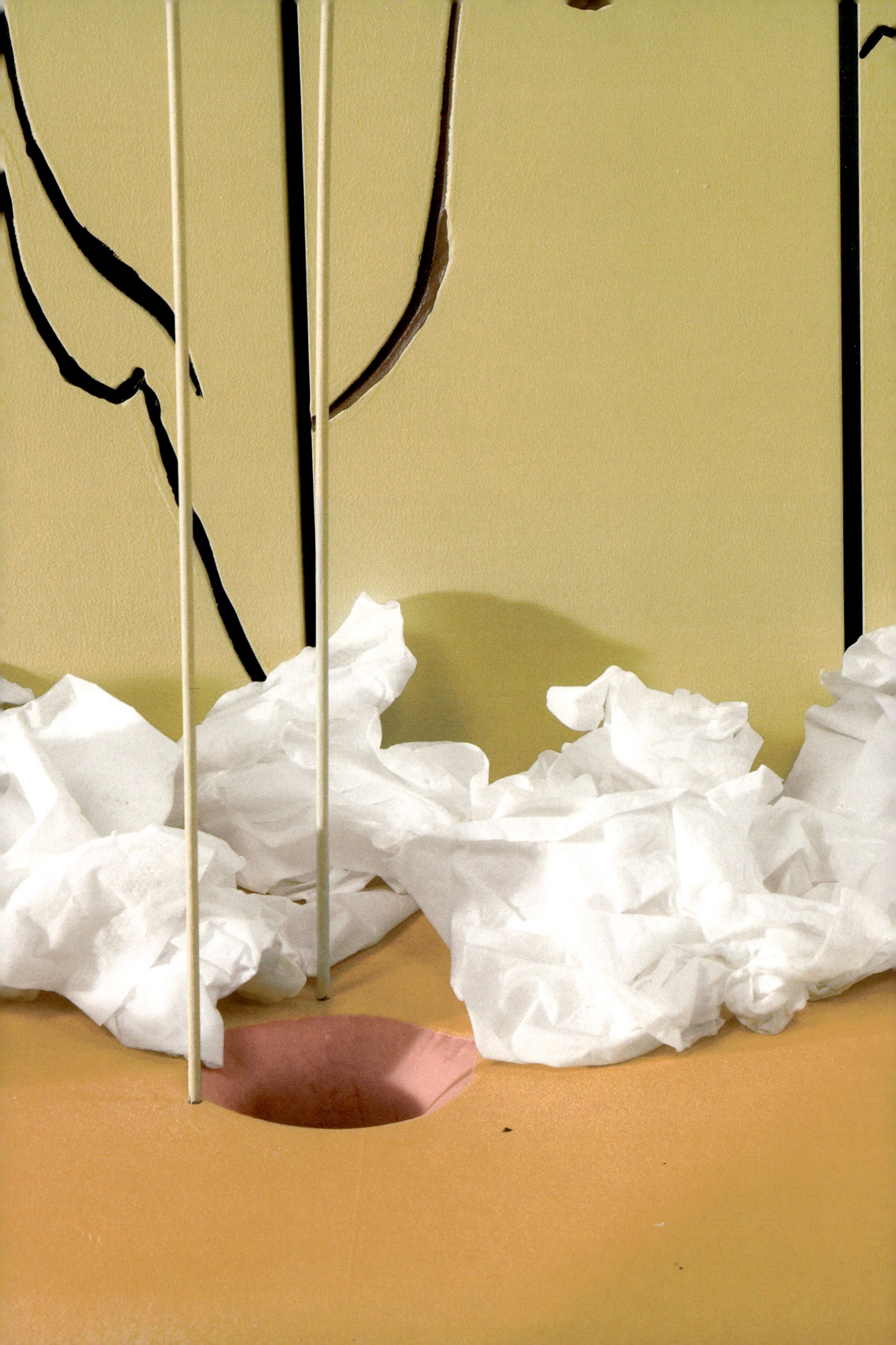

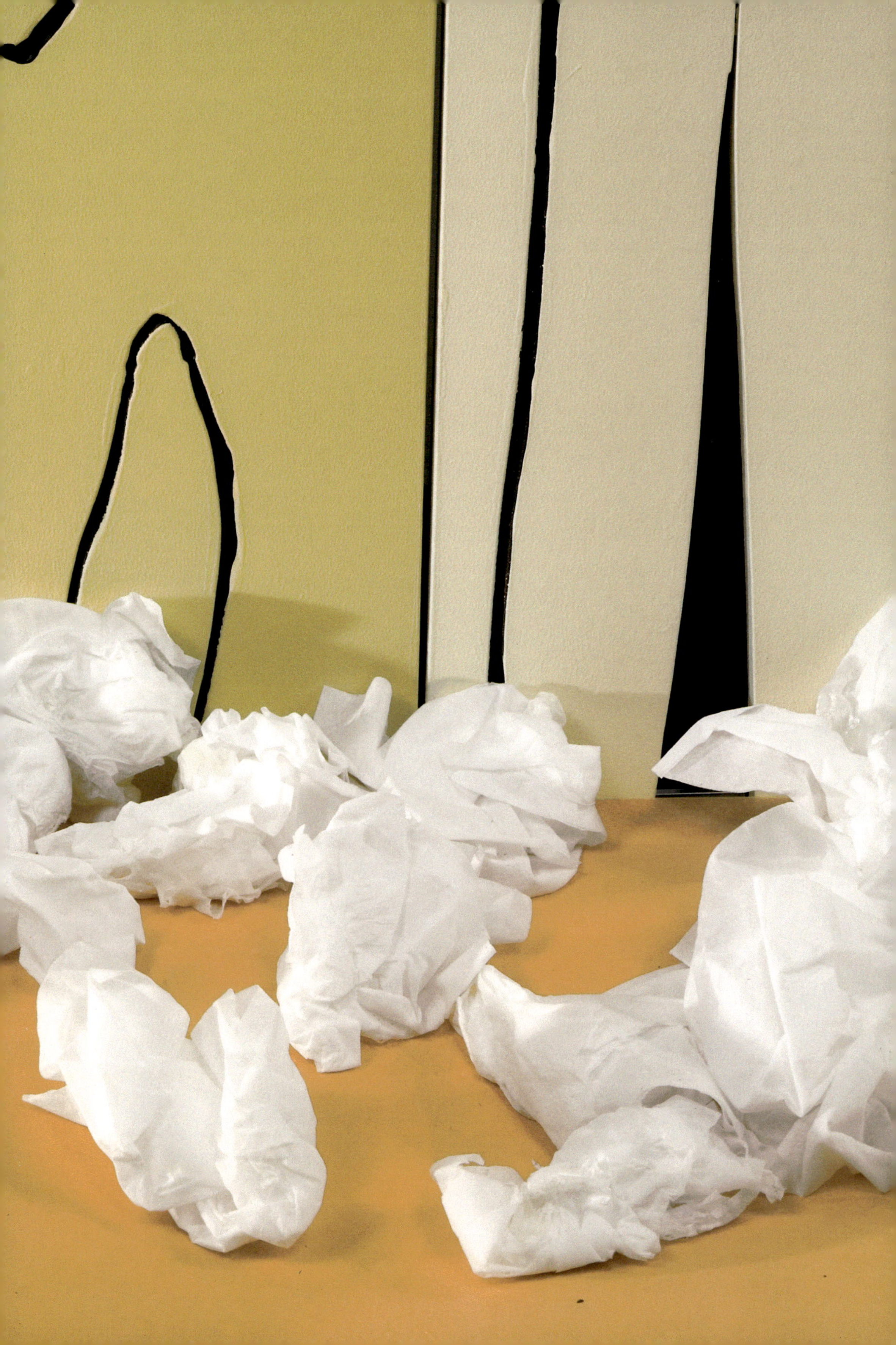

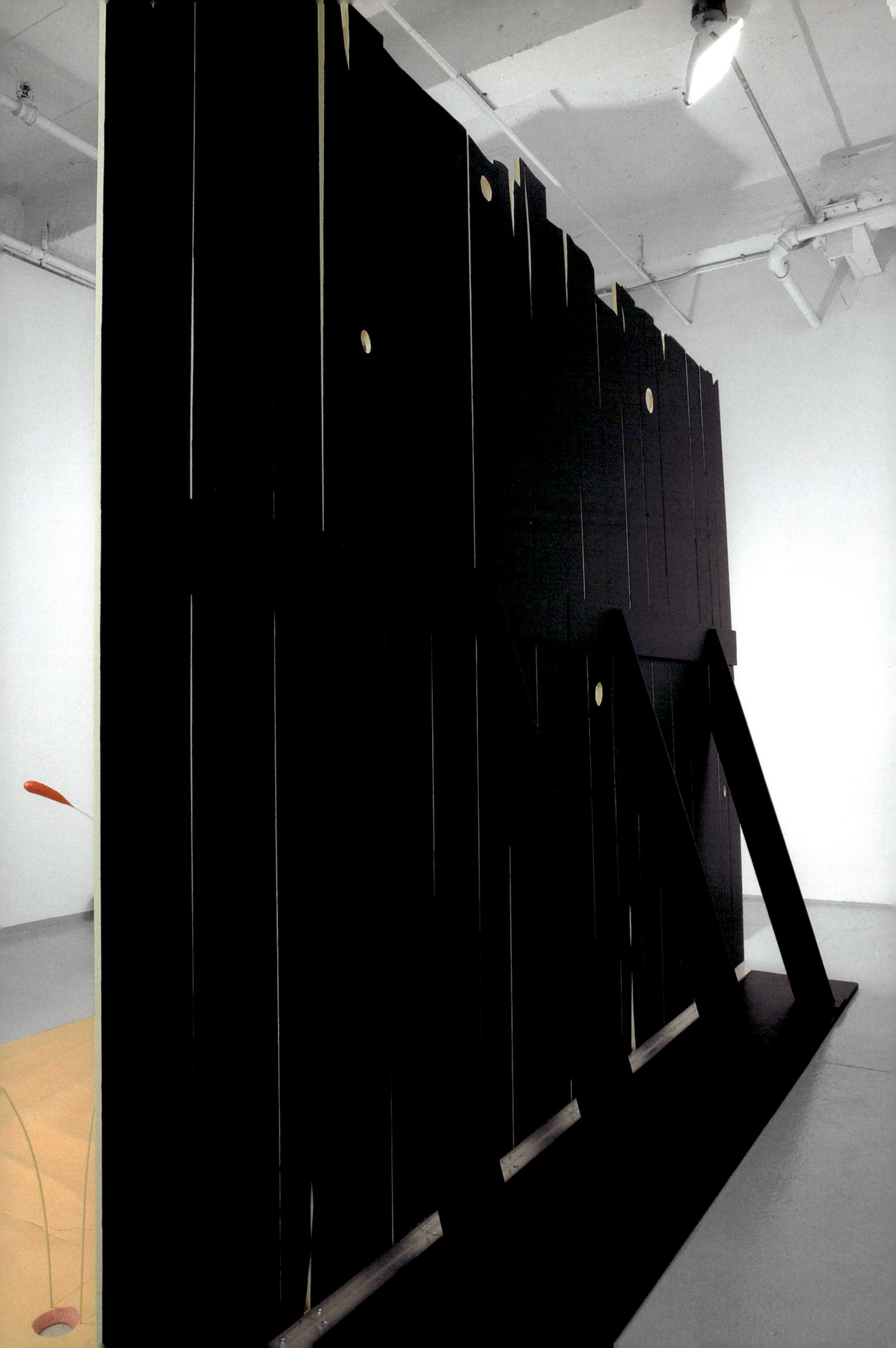

YOY ARE A
LYING SHIT
HATE YOU

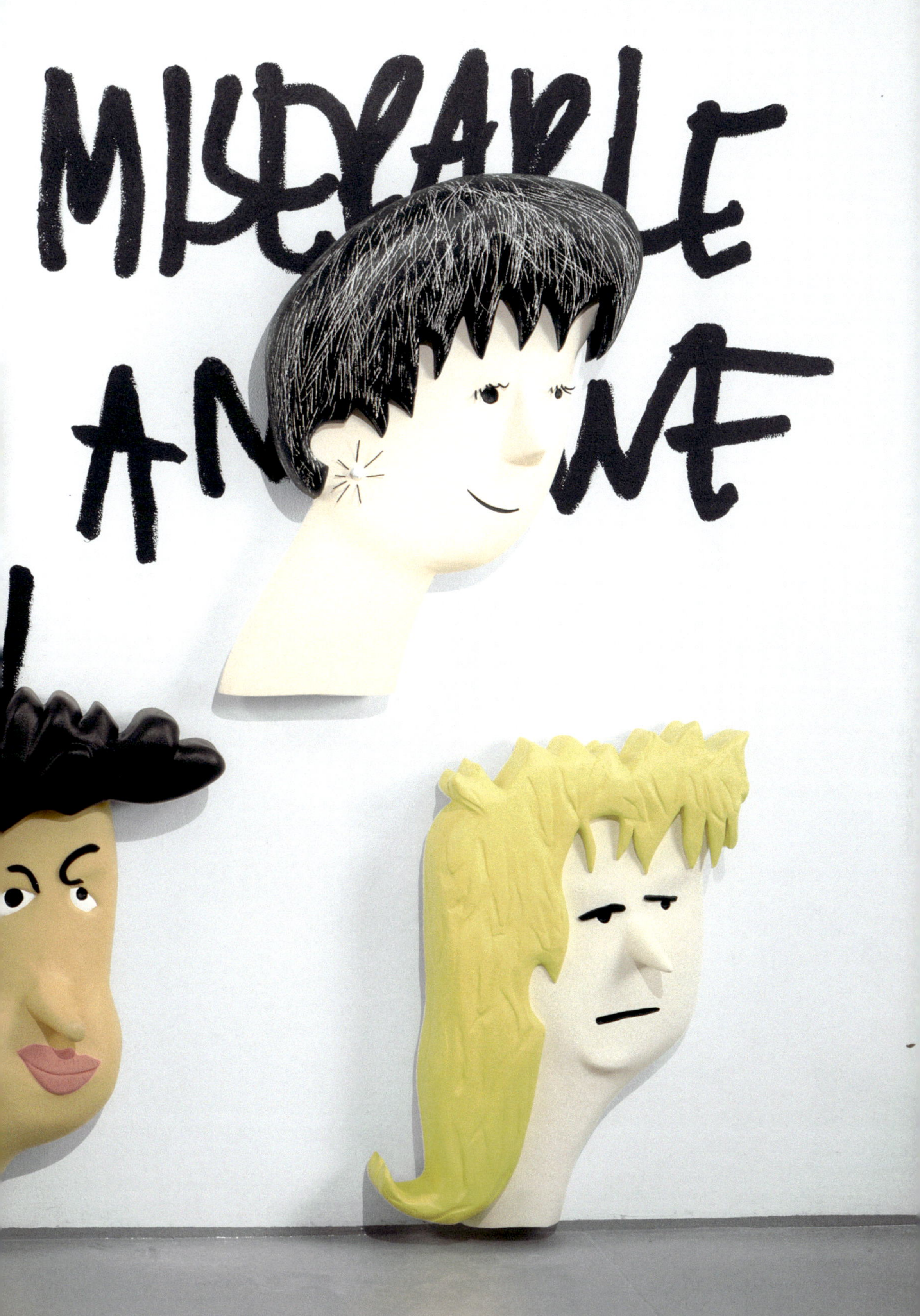
MISERABLE
ANYONE

Oh My God What Are We Gonna Do?!

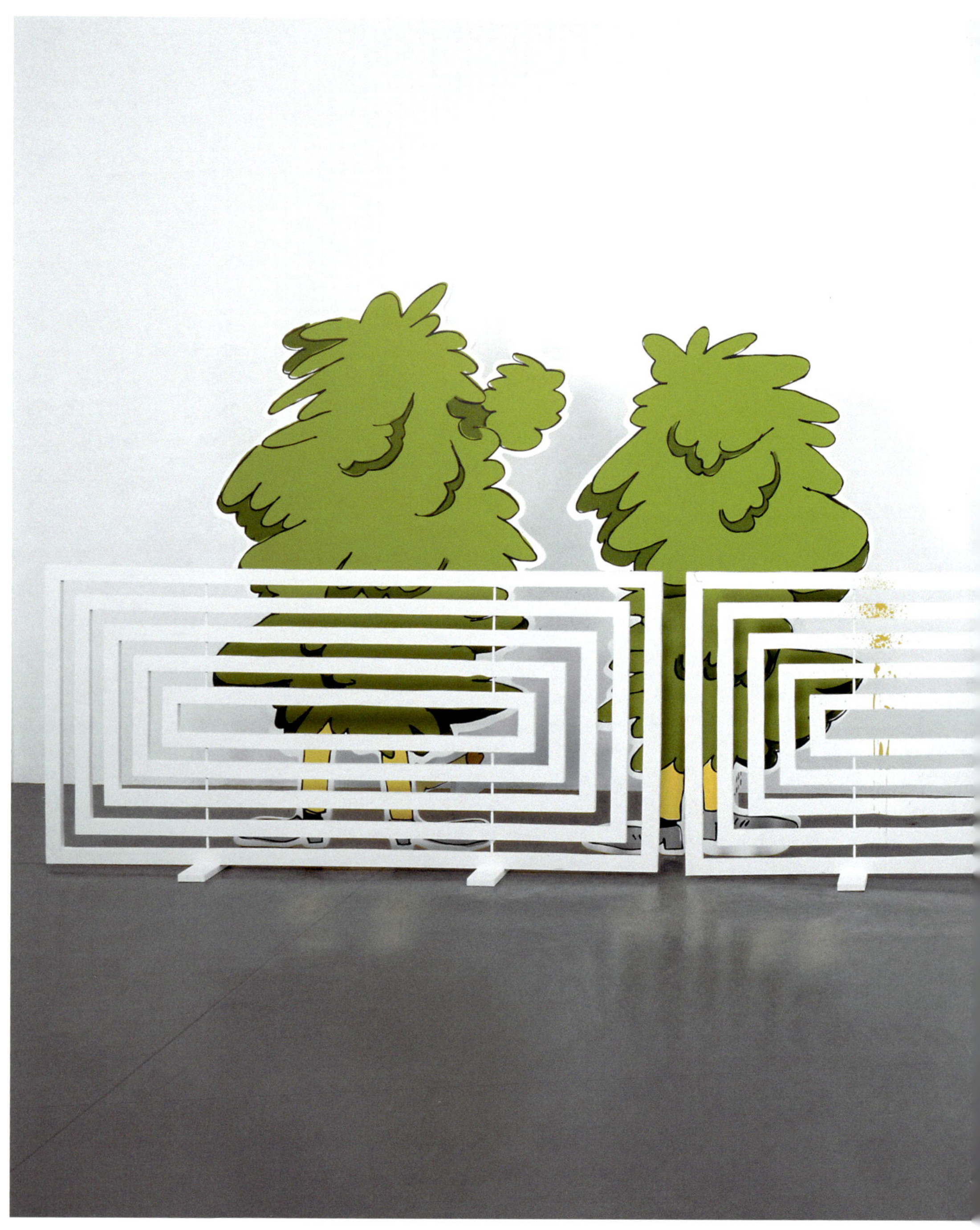

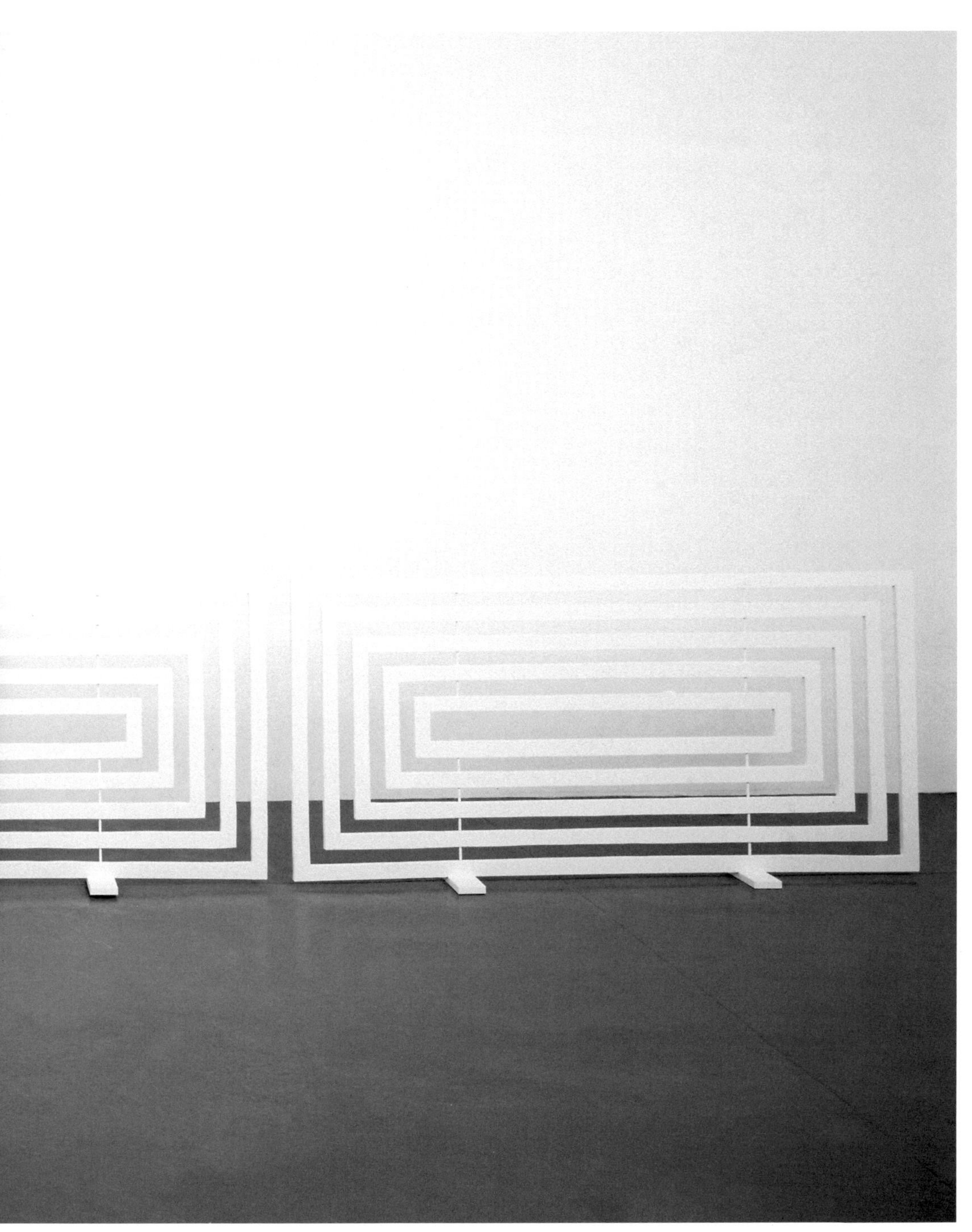

  Ground Surveillance Love Fruition with Farticles, 2005

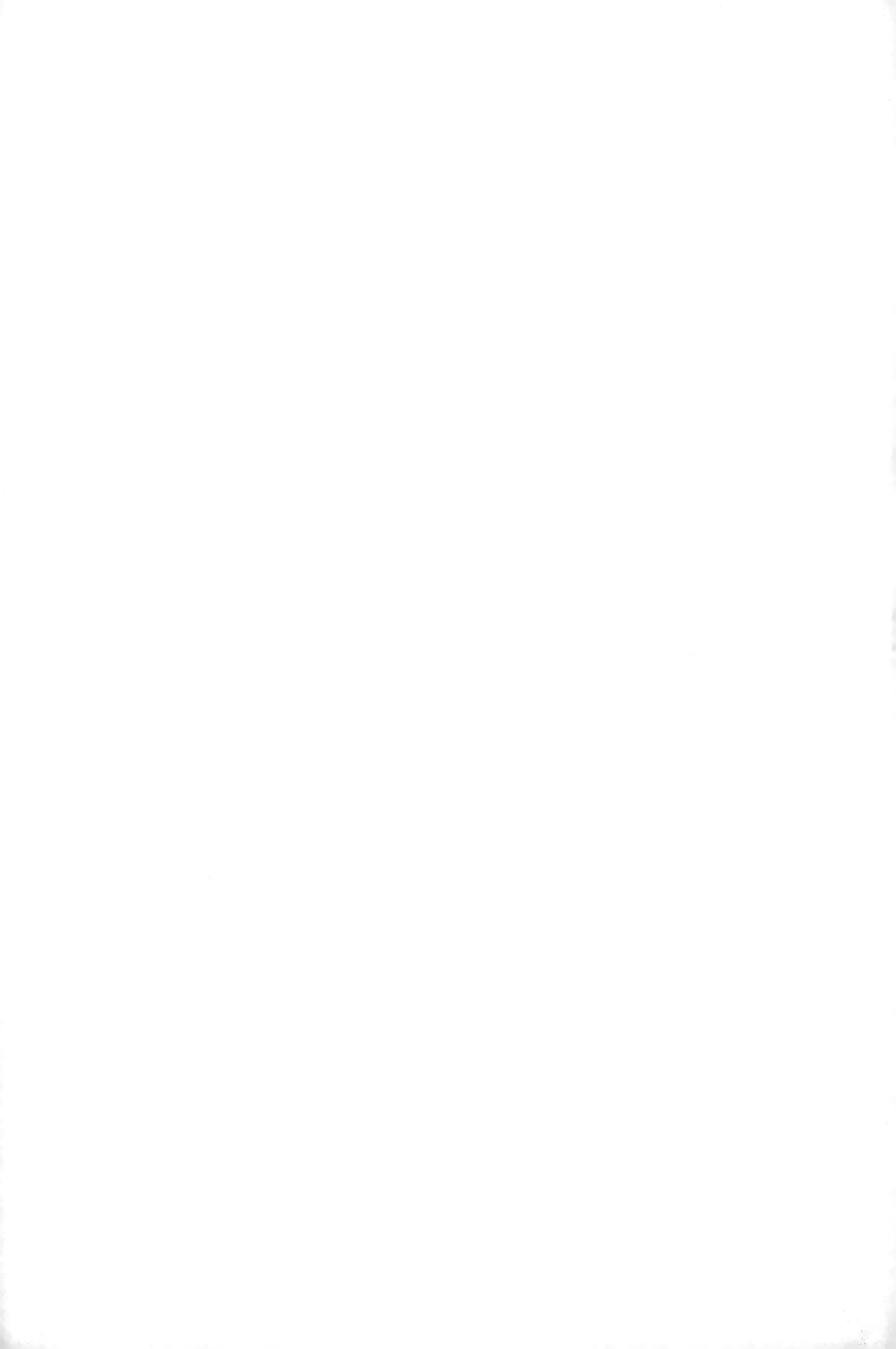

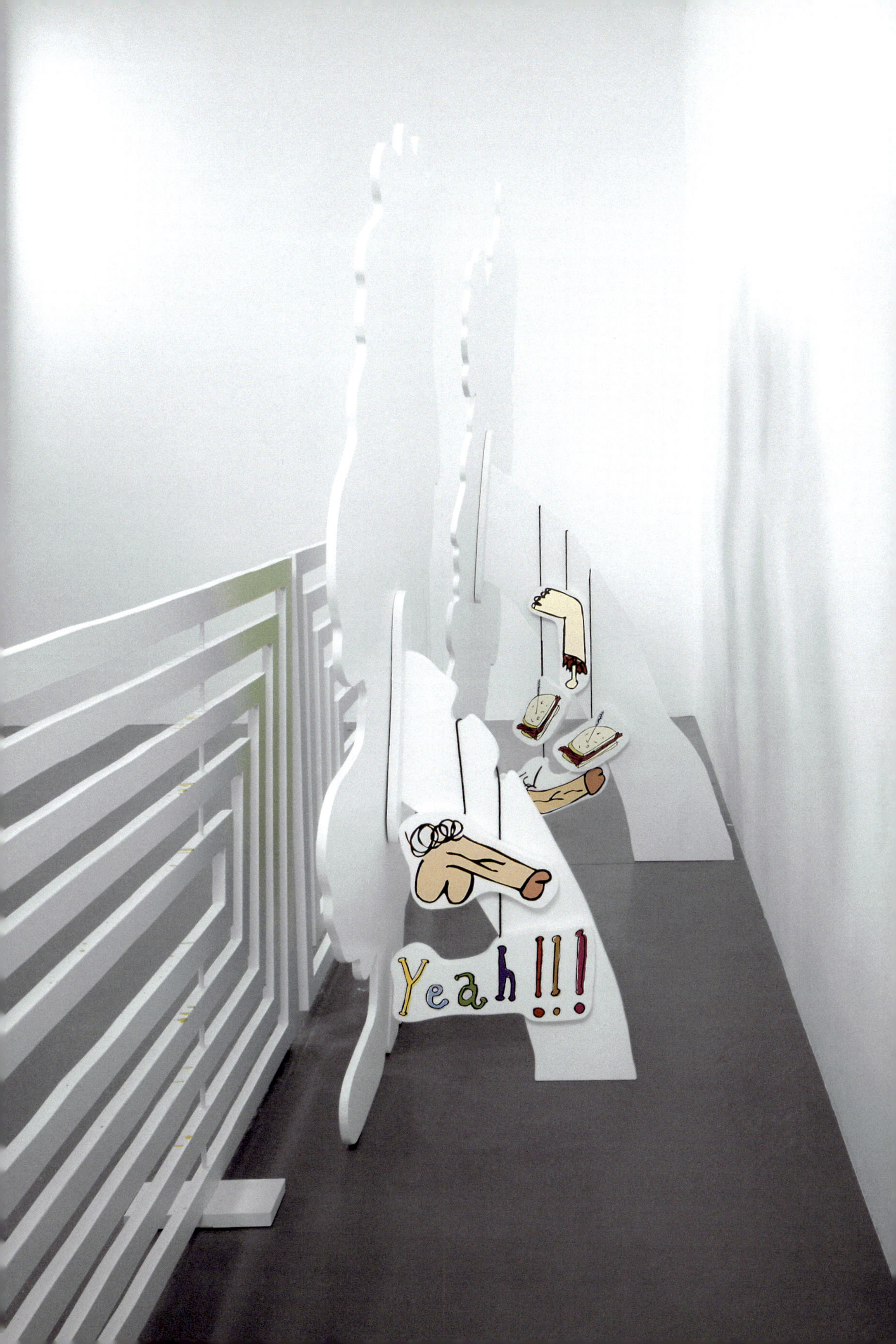
Yeah!!!

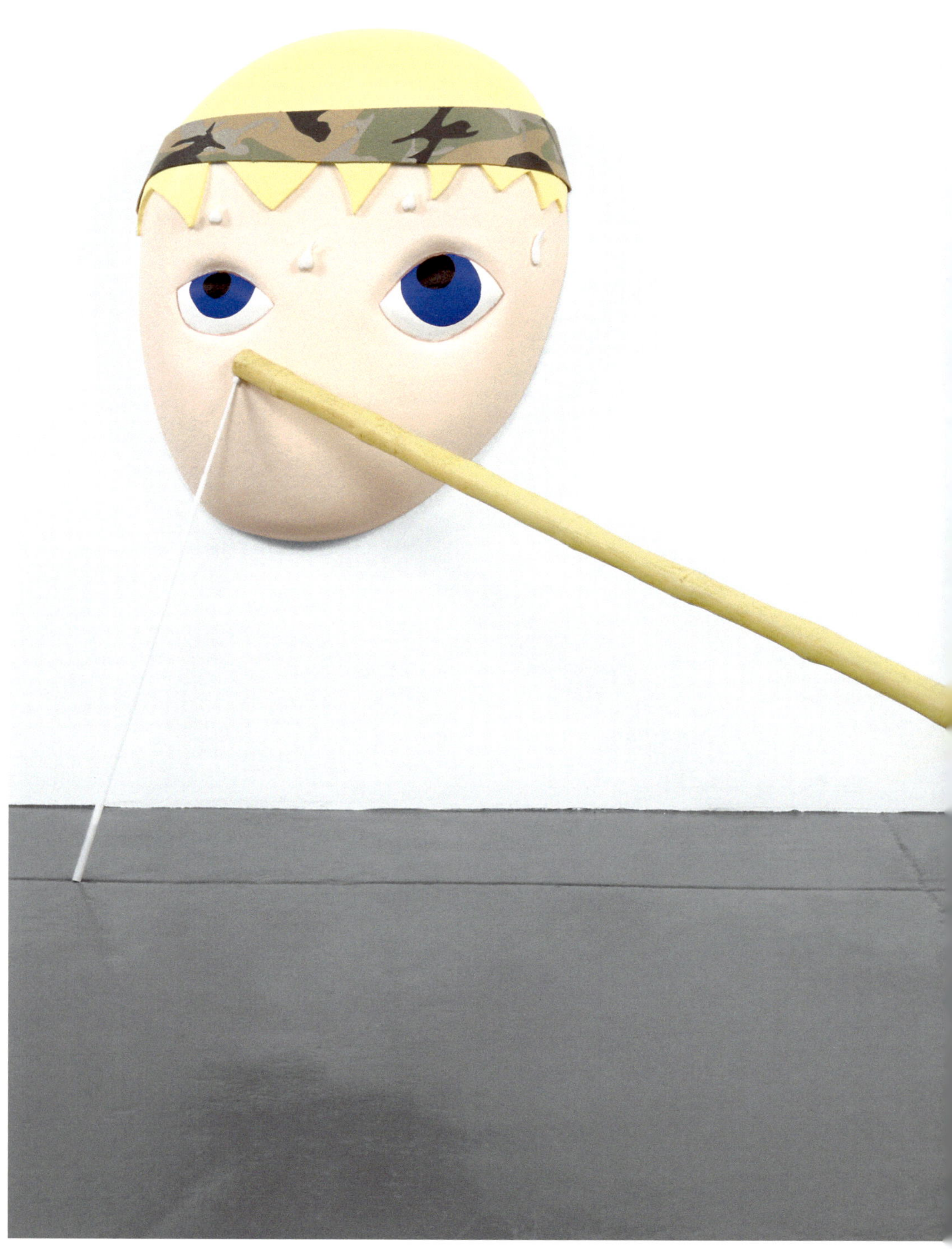

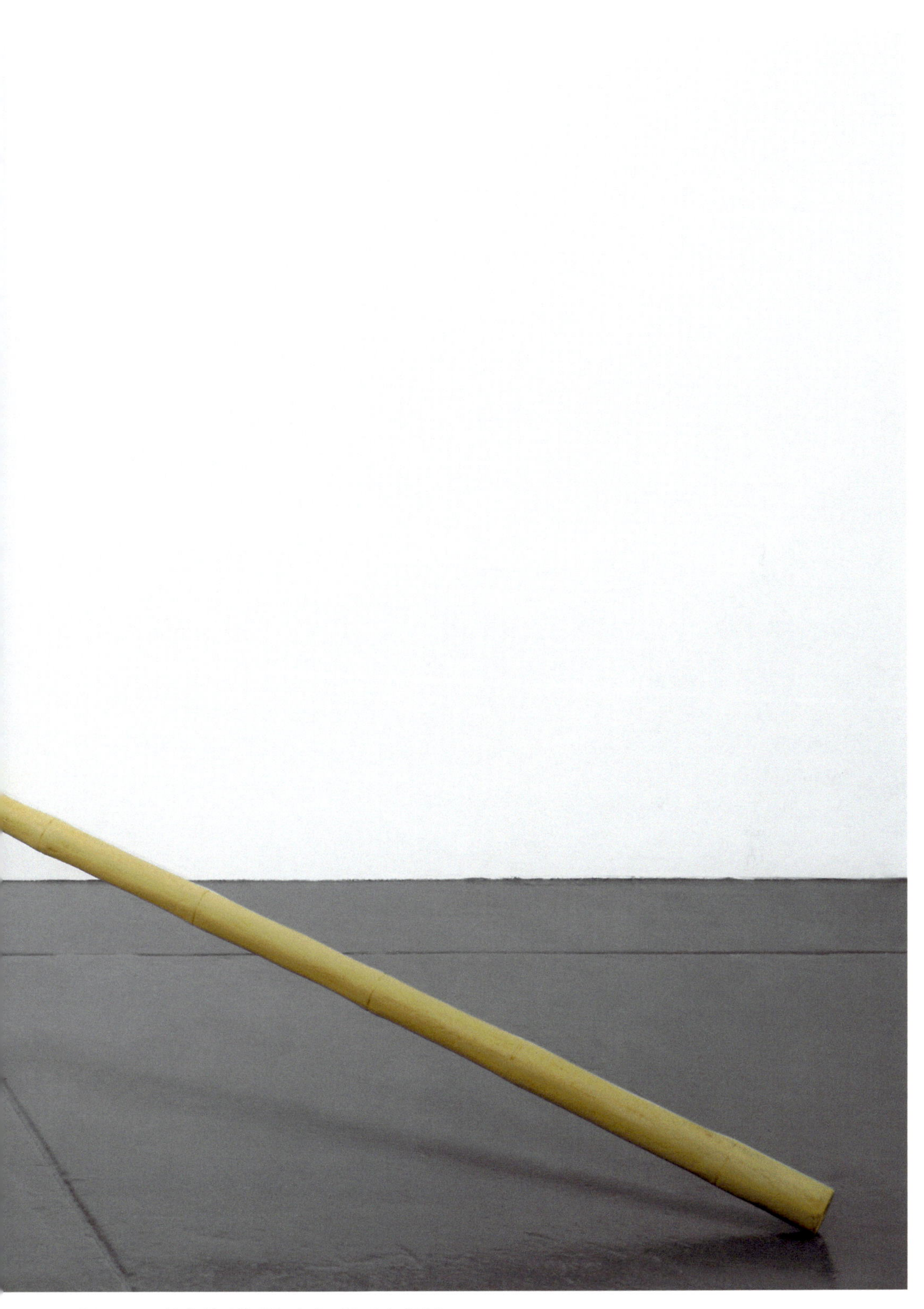

85 *Hell No We Won't Go/Facial*, 2005

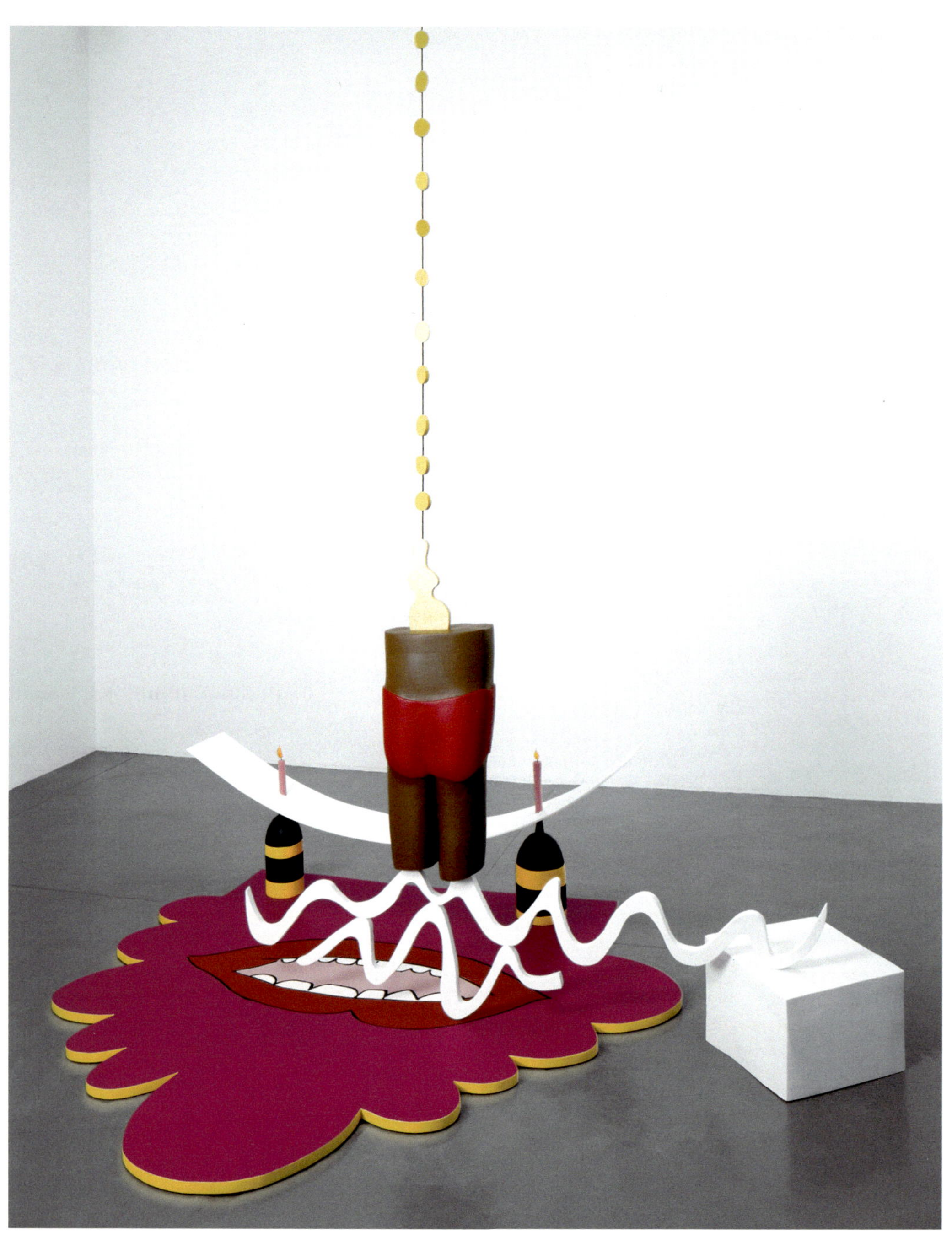

     Please Don't Bend, Fold, Spindle or Mutilate Me, 2005

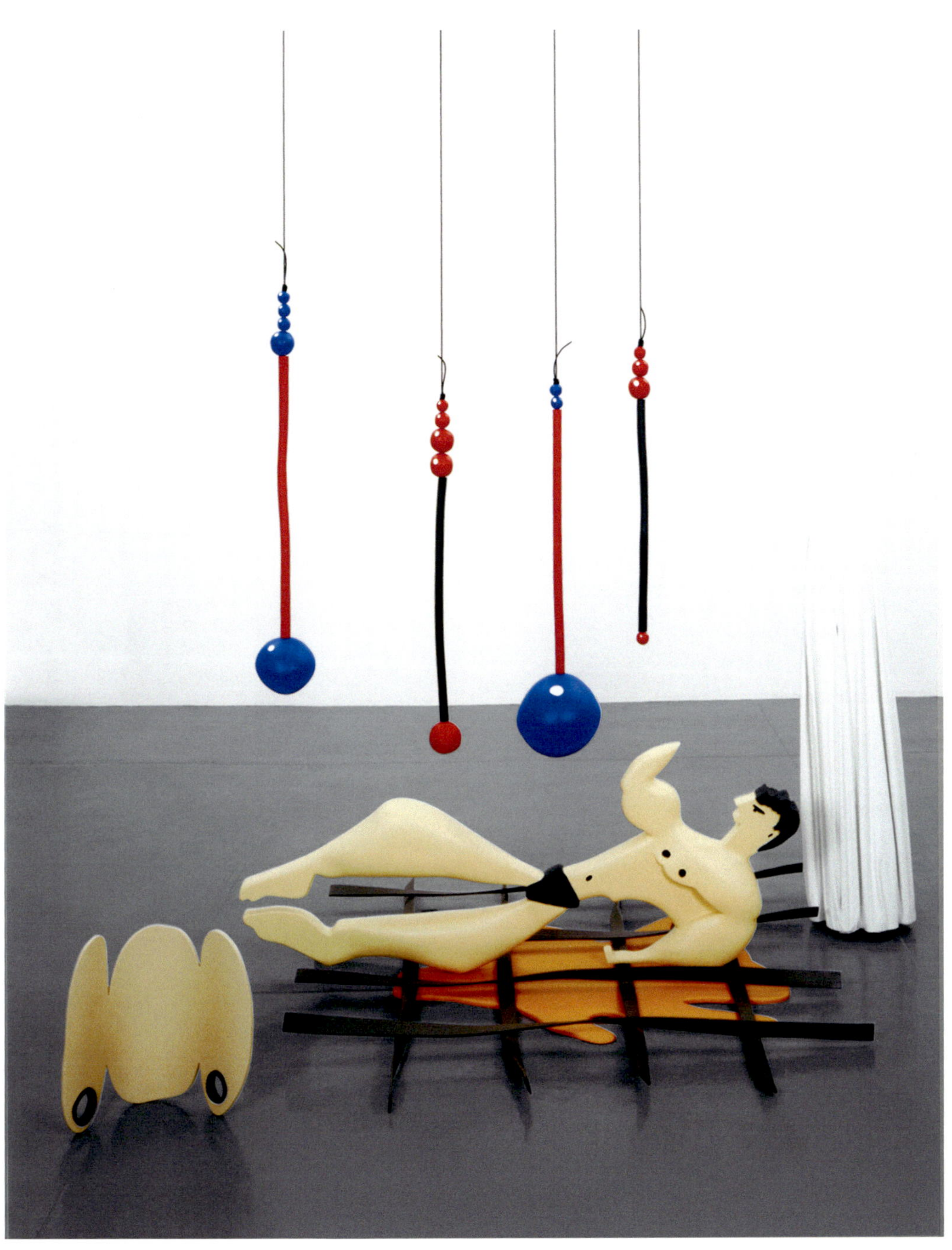

87   *Medevac Flashback…Therapy… Anal Leakage*, 2005

Shine The Light

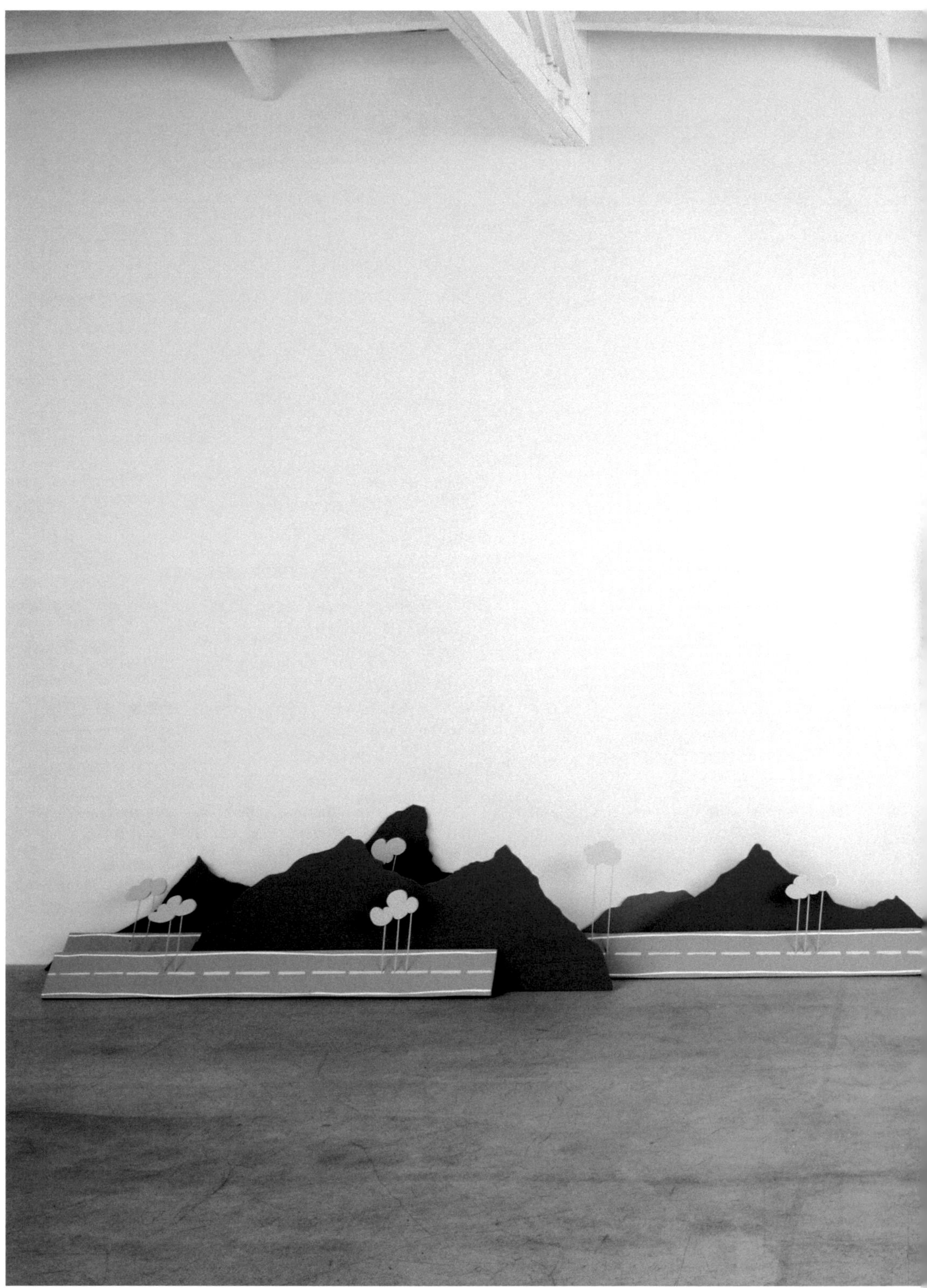

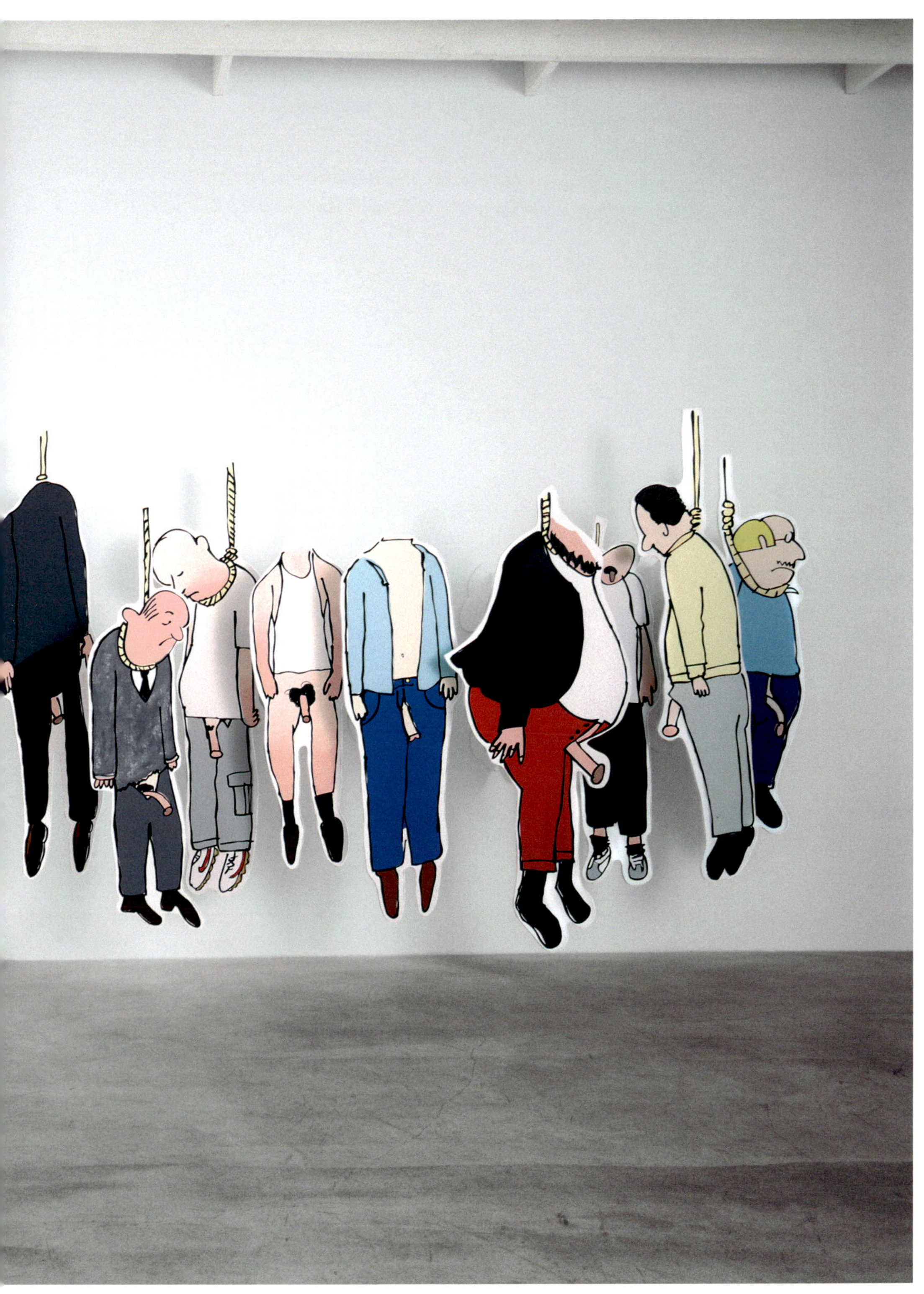

     Falling… Spilling… Sprawling…, 2005

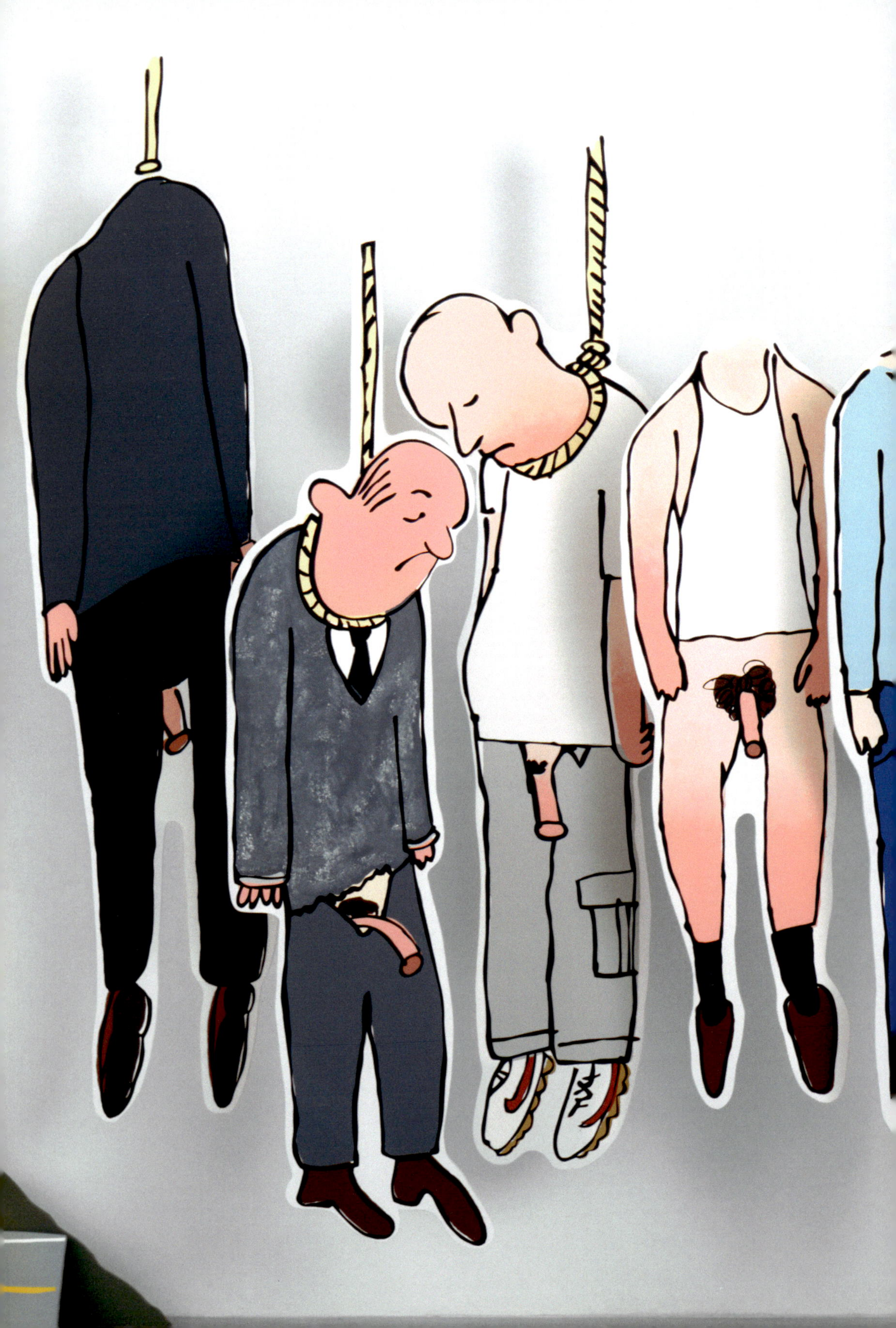

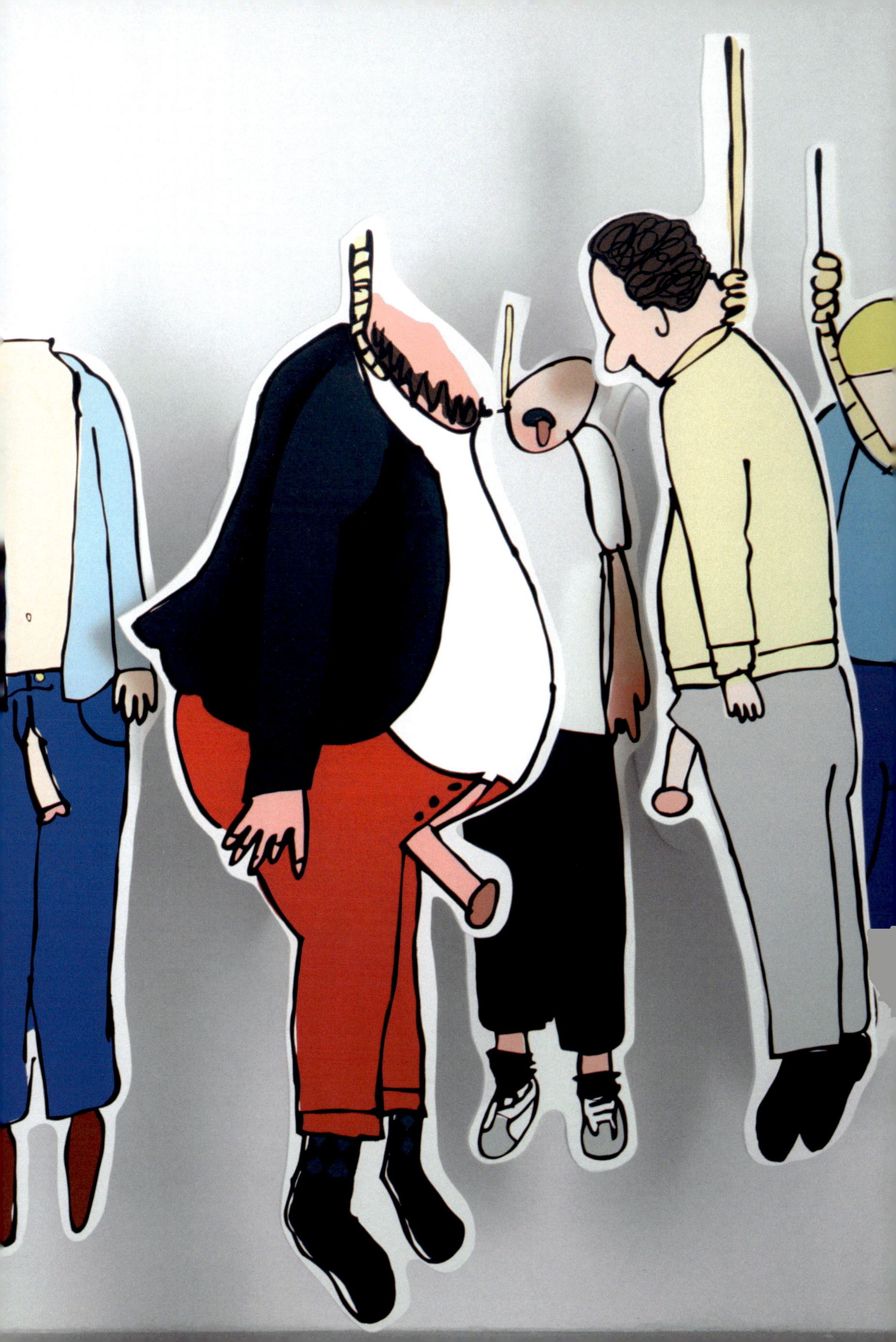

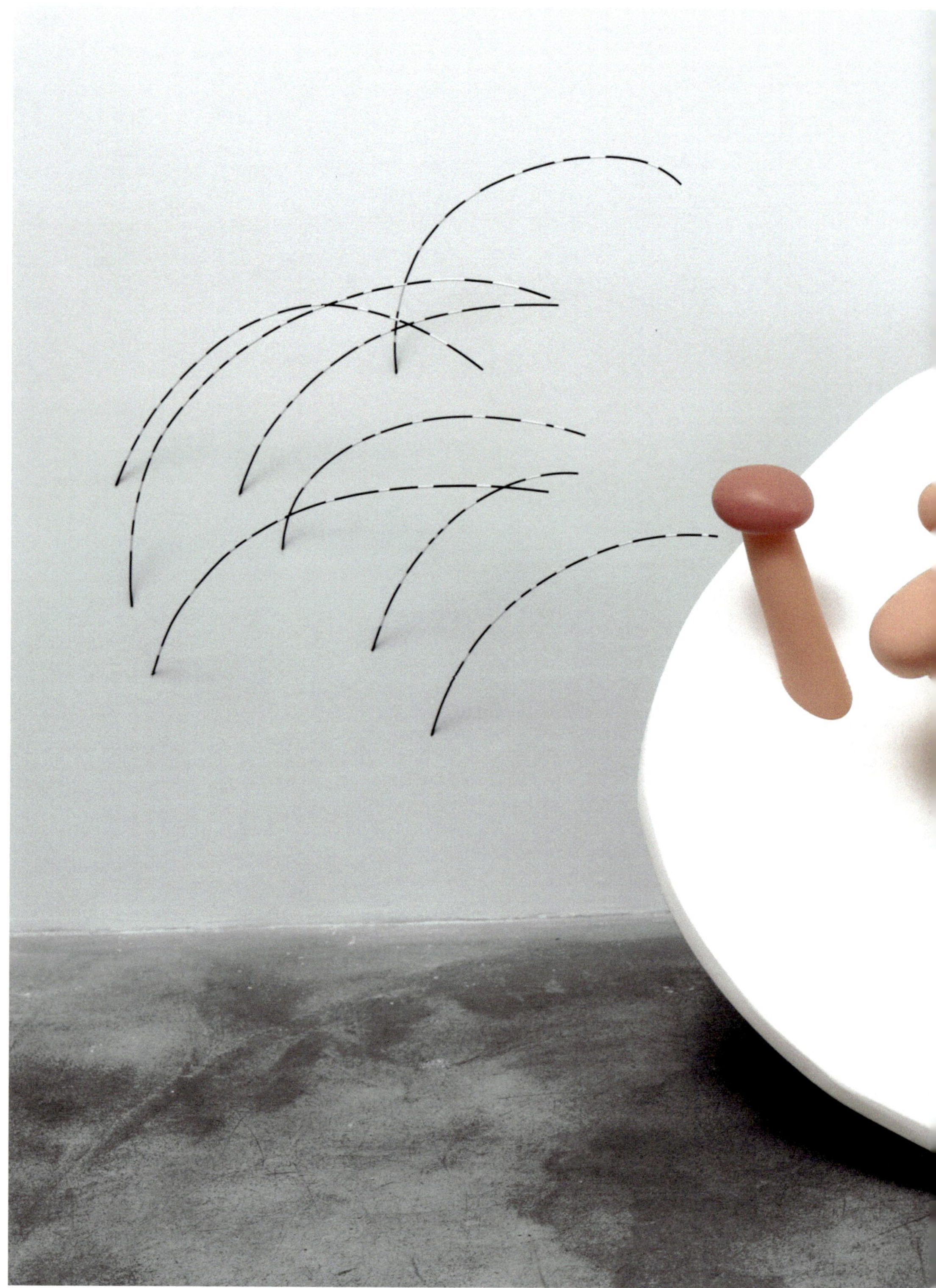

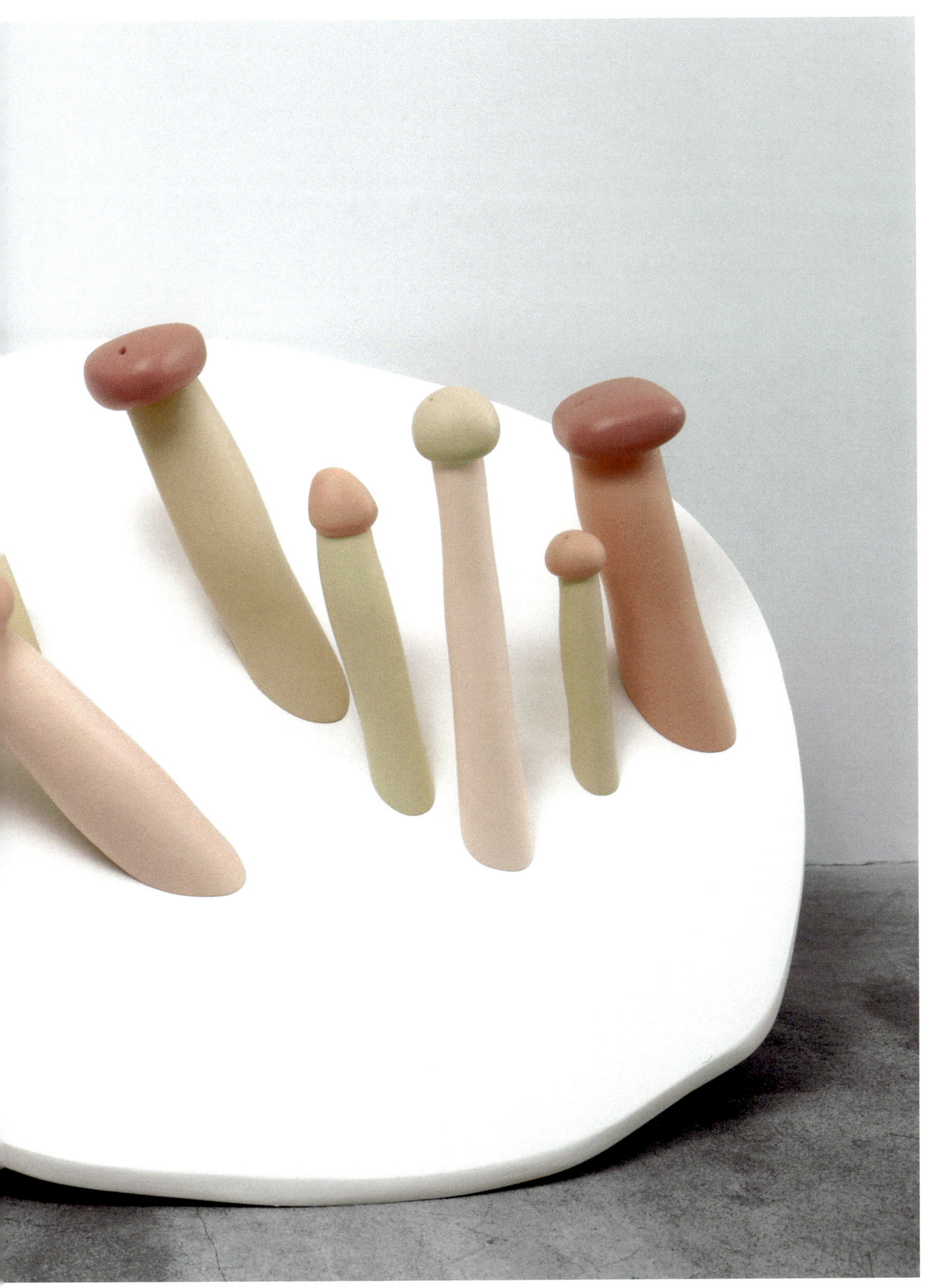

95   *Peed/Cummed On*, 2005

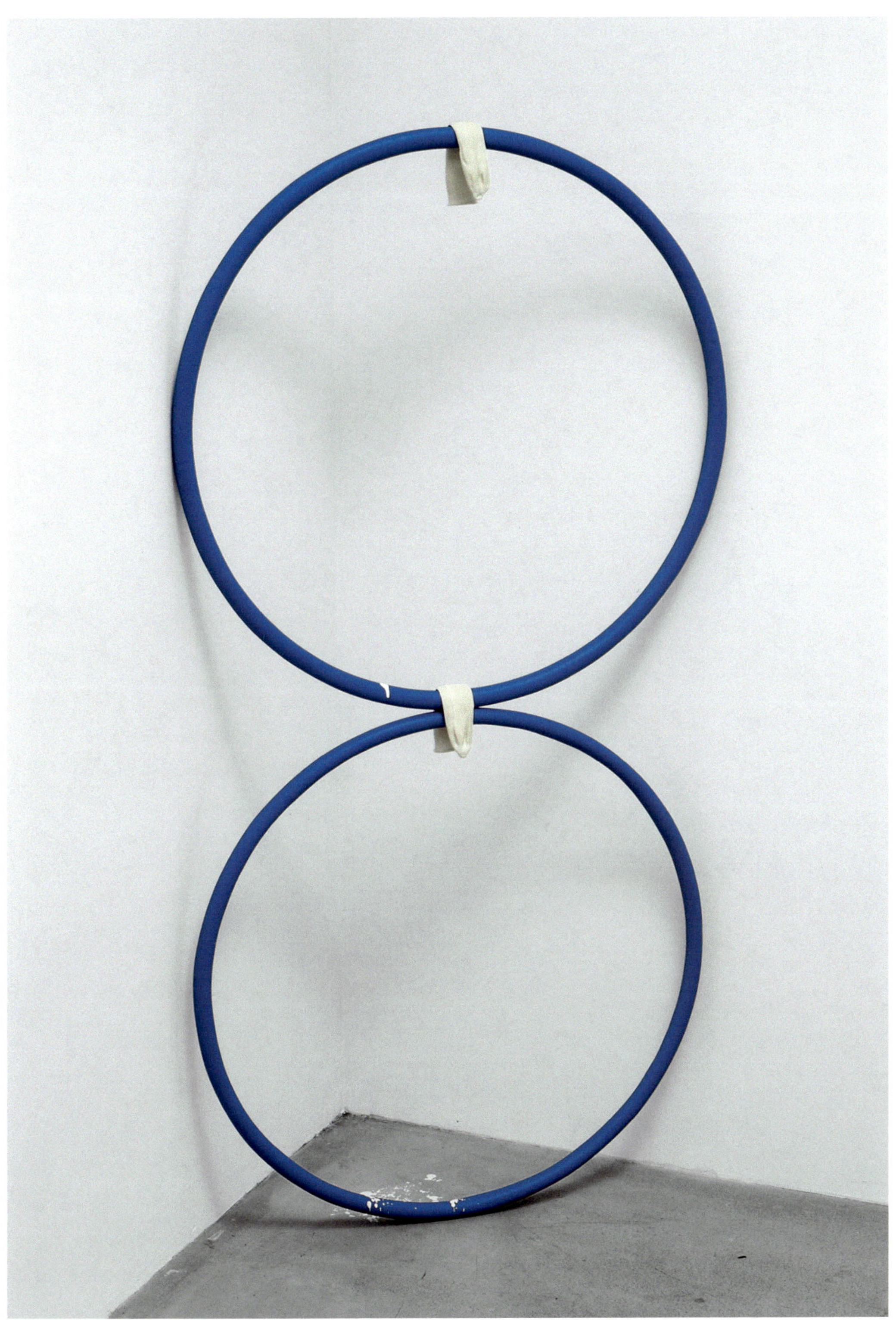

97   *Wiping Away Drips Obsolete*, 2005

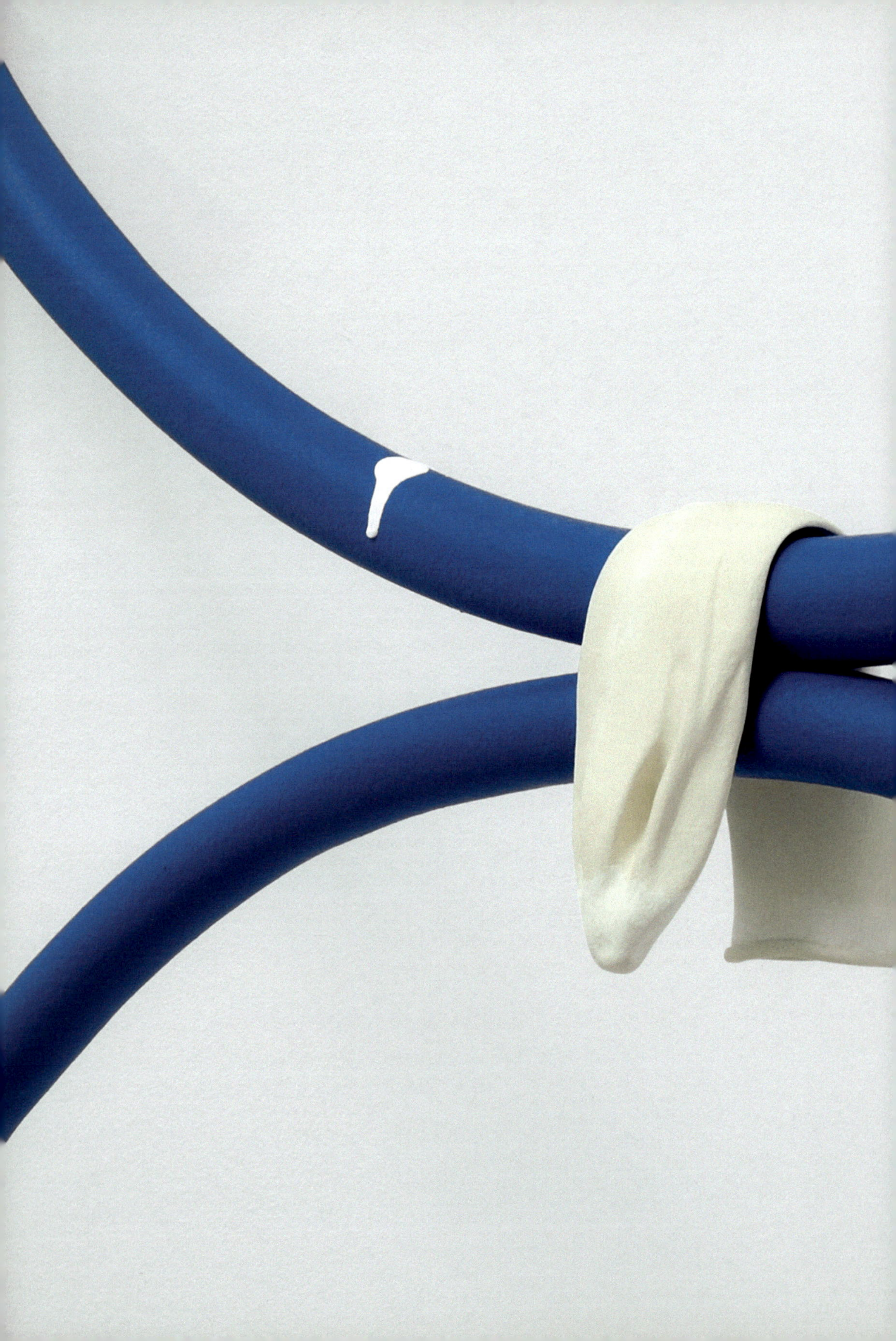

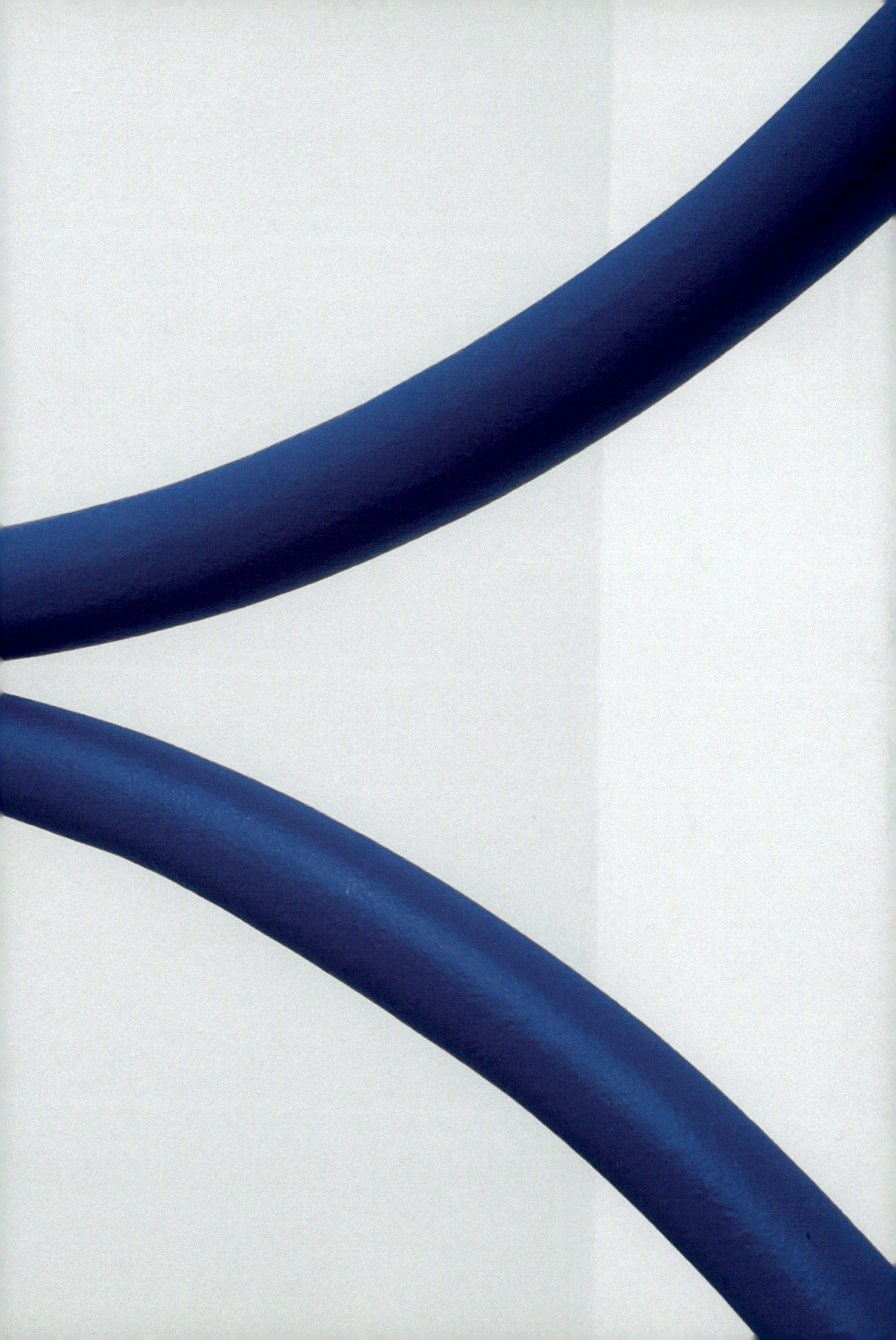

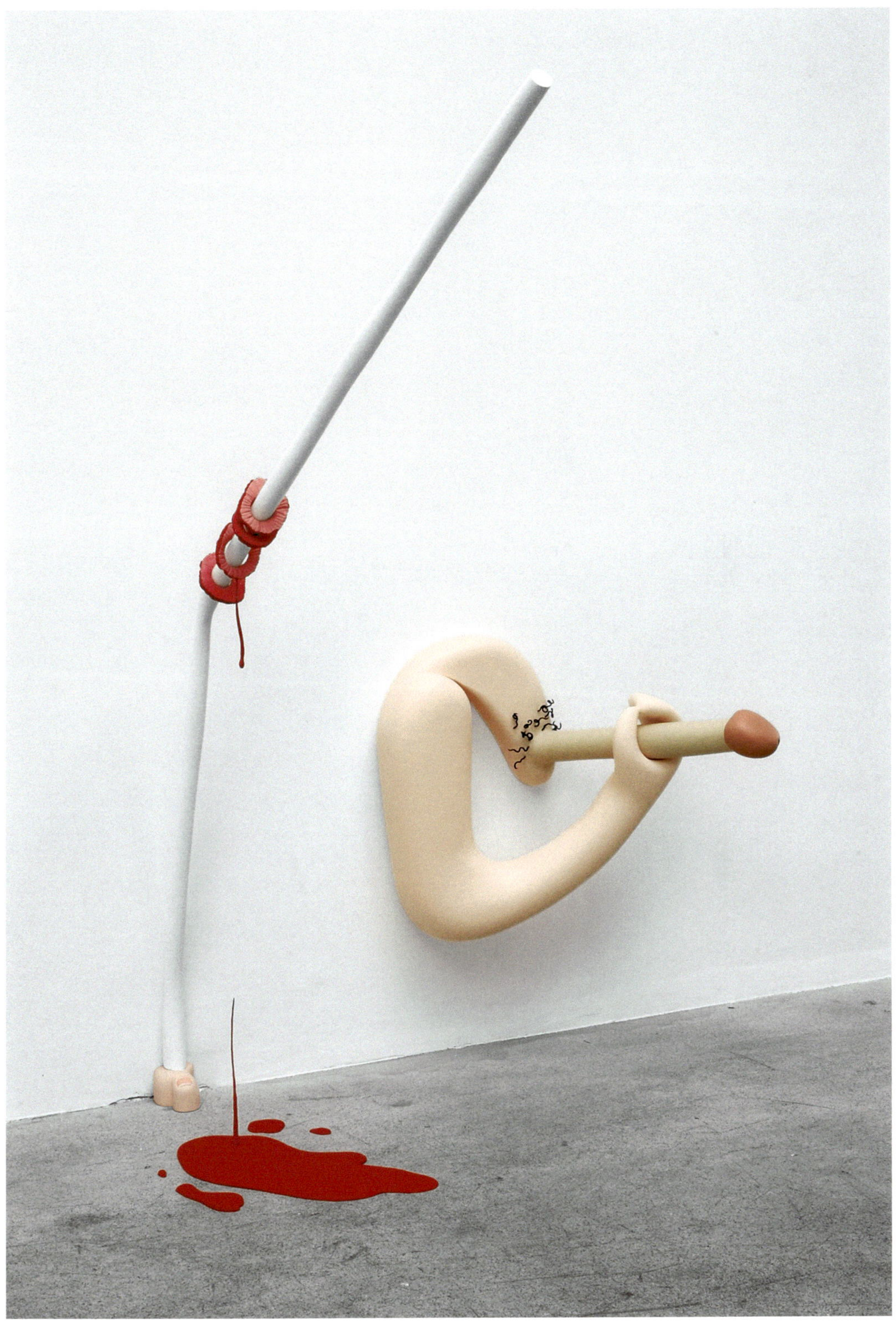

101　　*Rims*, 2005

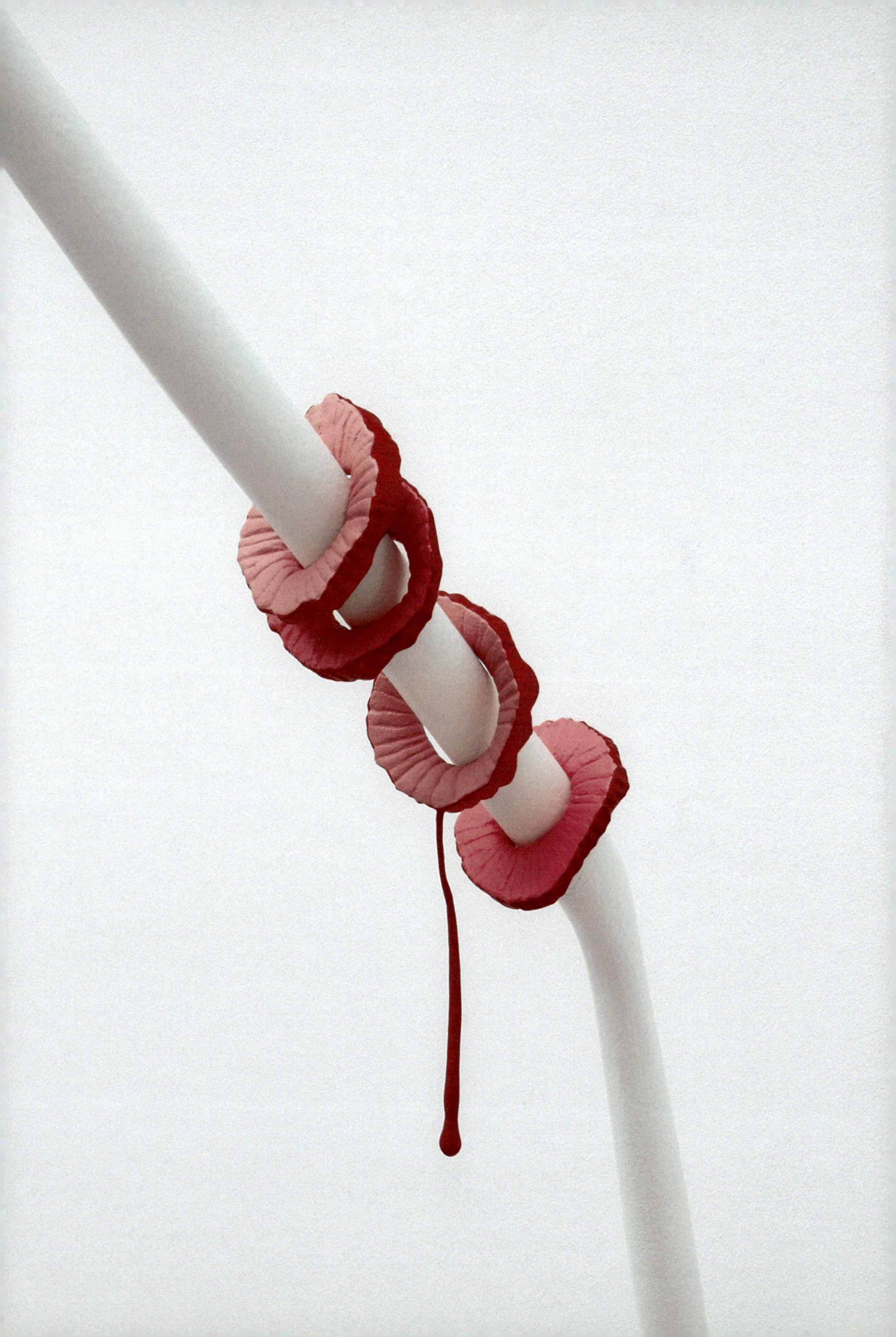

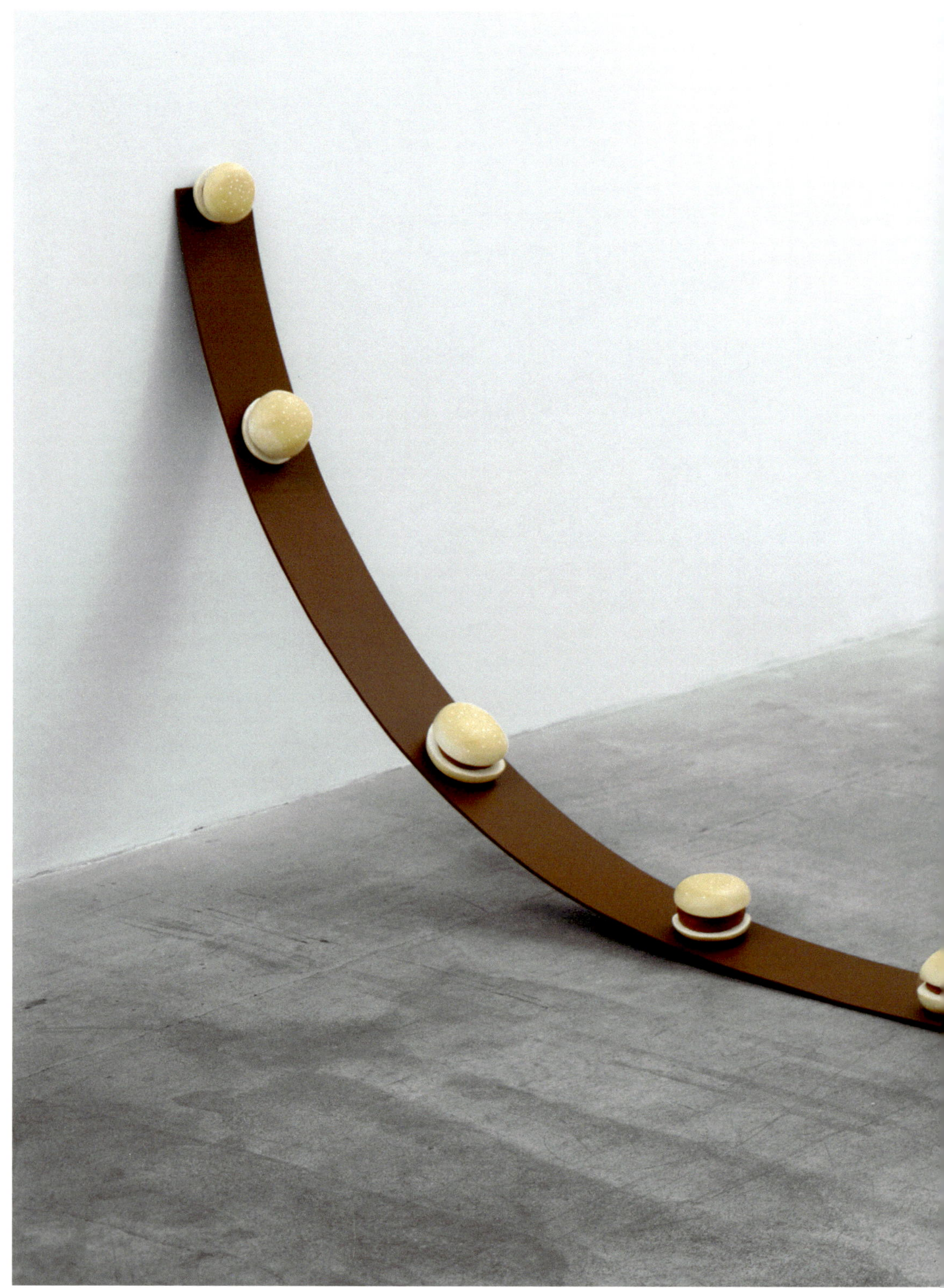

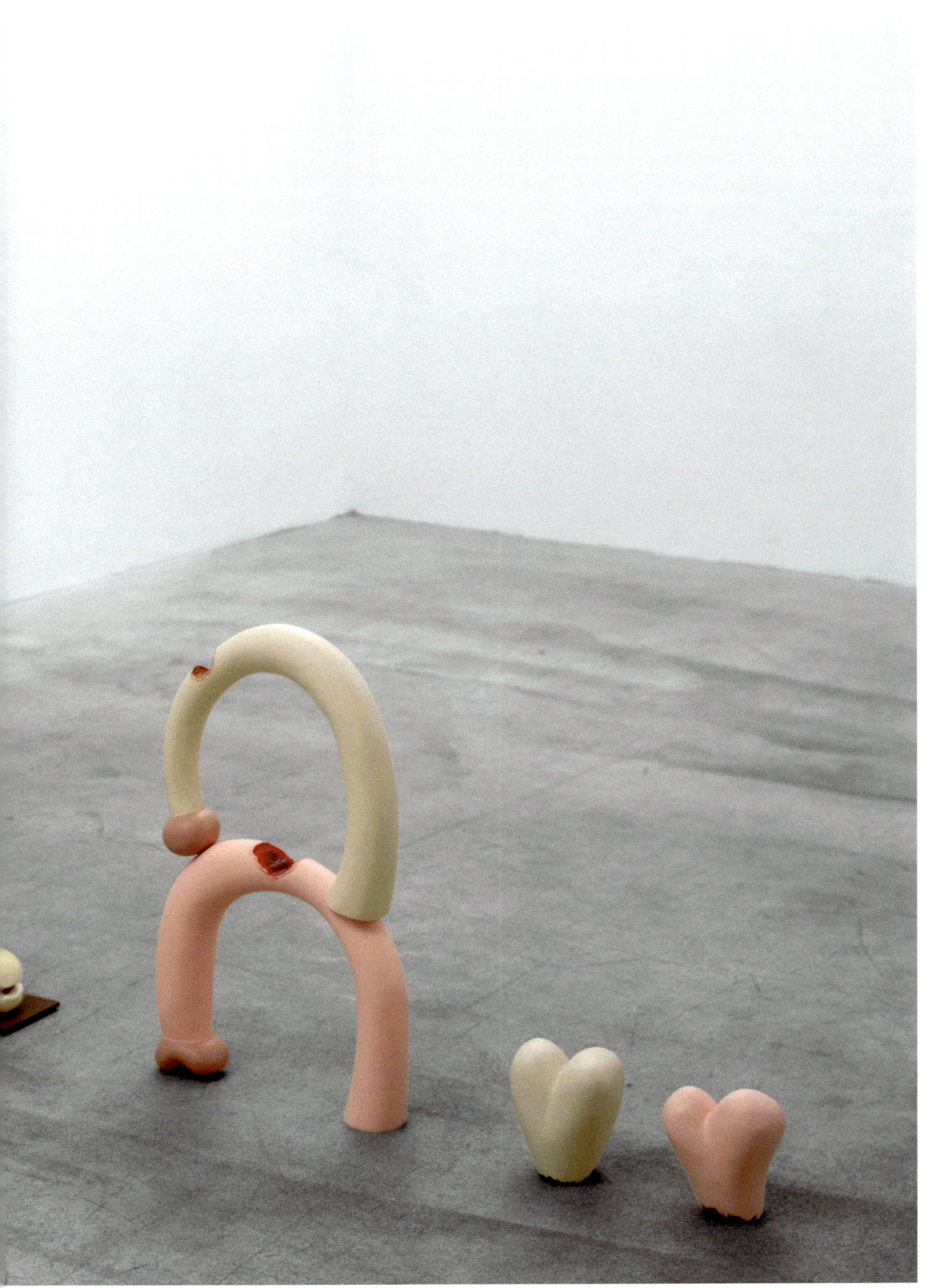

105   *Obese Eclipsed Cock*, 2005

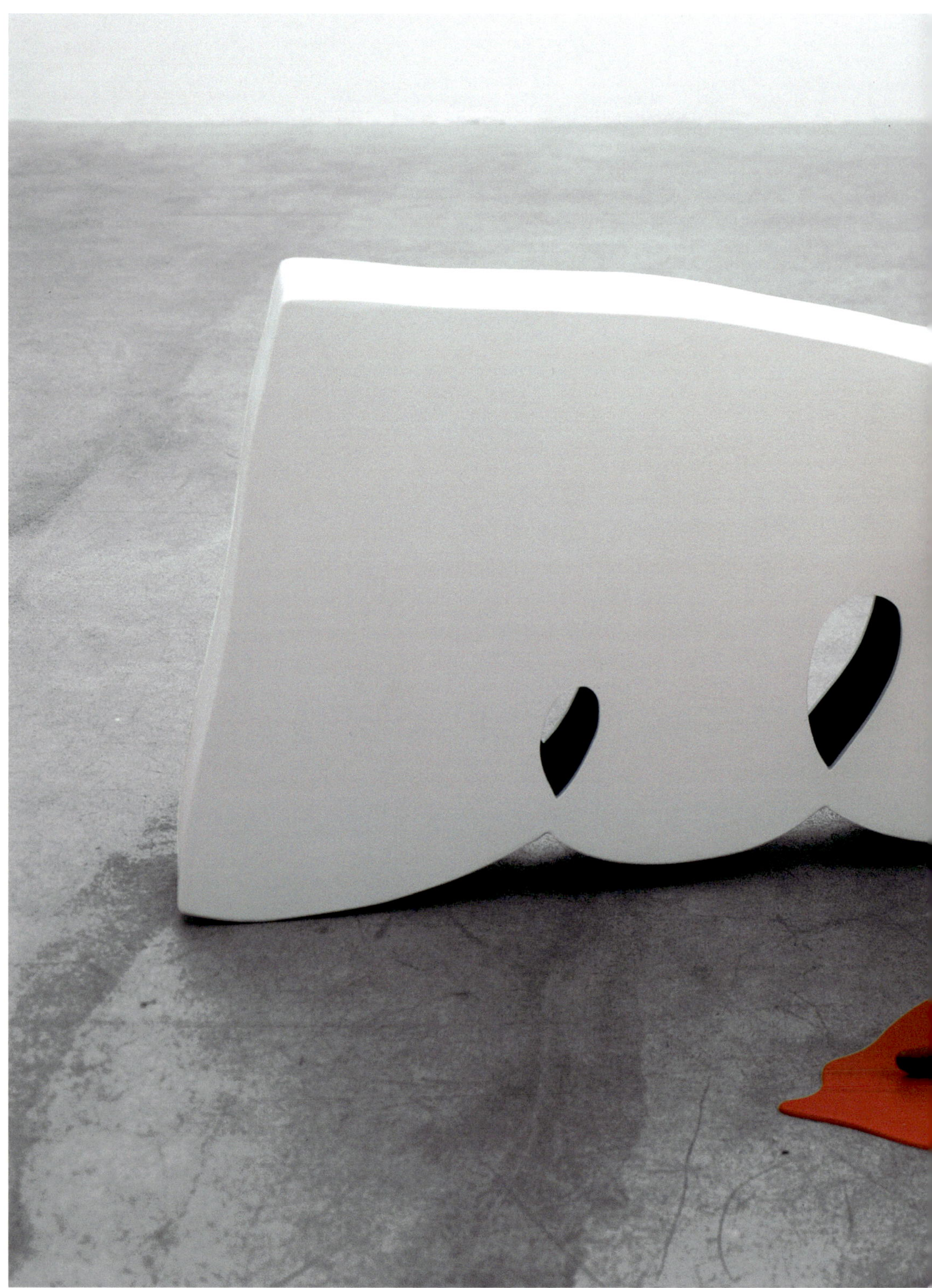

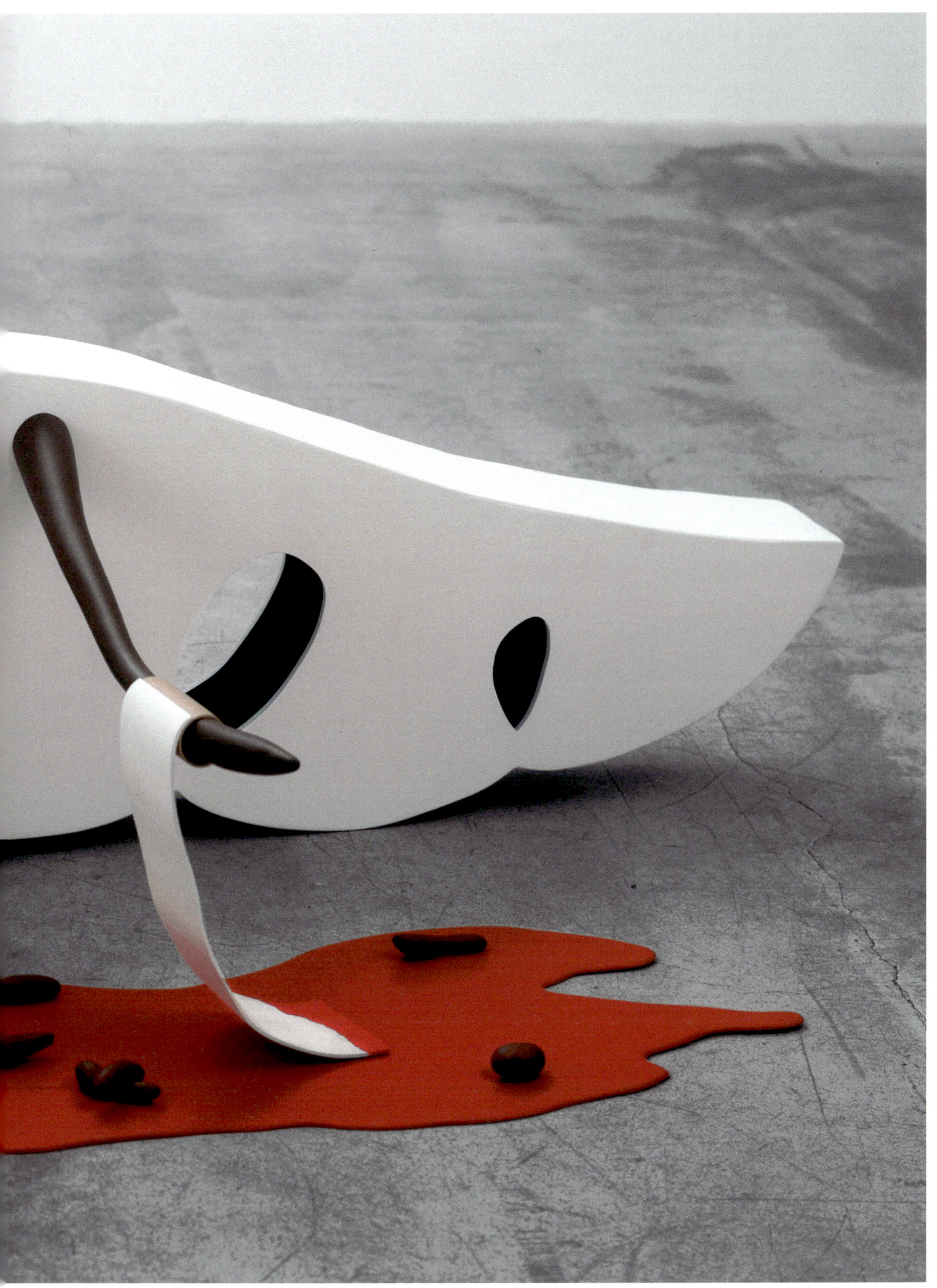

107   *Gate Open*, 2005

LIST OF WORKS

THREE-DIMENSIONAL OBJECTS (Height precedes width precedes depth)

Don't Have To, Period

54   *To Possess It, One Must Walk Through It At Night*, 2006
MDF, wood, steel, Masonite, plastic bags, cotton, paper, resin
325 x 731 x 220 cm (128 x 288 x 87 in)
Courtesy Andrea Rosen Gallery, New York

64   *Officer, Officer, Officer, Officer!*, 2006
MDF, wood, steel, plastic bags, paint
193 x 230 x 161 cm (76 x 90 x 64 in)
Courtesy Andrea Rosen Gallery, New York

68   *Don't Stop... Don't Stop the Feelin'*, 2006
MDF, steel, copper, aluminum, tissue, glue, paint
225 x 281 x 335 cm (88 x 110 x 132 in)
Courtesy Andrea Rosen Gallery, New York

Oh My God What Are We Gonna Do?!

80   *Ground Surveillance Love Fruition with Farticles*, 2005
MDF, aluminum, string, paint
Variable width: 174 x 542 x 100 cm (68 x 213 x 39 in) as 3 fences,
174 x 908 x 100 cm (68 x 357 x 39 in) as 5 fences
Private Collection, Madrid, Spain
Courtesy Vacio 9, Madrid, and Andrea Rosen Gallery, New York

84   *Hell No We Won't Go/Facial*, 2005
MDF, canvas, wood, copper, paint
65 x 97 x 77 cm (25 x 38 x 30 in)
Private Collection, Cantabria, Spain
Courtesy Vacio 9, Madrid, and Andrea Rosen Gallery, New York

86   *Please Don't Bend, Fold, Spindle or Mutilate Me*, 2005
MDF, aluminum, wood, string, steel, paint
Height variable x 234 x 175 cm (variable x 94 x 69 in)
Private Collection, Madrid, Spain
Courtesy Vacio 9, Madrid, and Andrea Rosen Gallery, New York

87   *Medevac Flashback...Therapy... Anal Leakage*, 2005
MDF, wood, string, cotton sheet, paint
Height variable x 178 x 140 cm (variable x 70 x 55 in)
Private Collection, Switzerland
Courtesy Vacio 9, Madrid, and Andrea Rosen Gallery, New York

Shine The Light

90   *Falling... Spilling... Sprawling...*, 2005
MDF, wood, paint, steel
Dimensions vary with installation. Each unit:
Hanging men: 198 x 305 x 51 cm (78 x 120 x 20 in)
Landscape element 01: 53 x 183 x 13 cm (21 x 72 x 5 in)
Landscape element 02: 57 x 207 x 13 cm (22 x 81 x 5 in)
Landscape element 03: 62 x 188 x 13 cm (24 x 74 x 5 in)
Landscape element 04: 29 x 74 x 13 cm (12 x 29 x 5 in)
Astrup Fearnley Collection, Oslo, Norway
Courtesy MARC FOXX, Los Angeles, and Andrea Rosen Gallery, New York

94   *Peed/Cummed On*, 2005
MDF, wood, steel, paint
84 x 180 x 81 cm (33 x 71 x 32 in)
Courtesy MARC FOXX, Los Angeles, and Andrea Rosen Gallery, New York

97   *Wiping Away Drips Obsolete*, 2005
Wood, paint
170 x 86 x 9 cm (67 x 34 x 3 in)
Courtesy MARC FOXX, Los Angeles, and Andrea Rosen Gallery, New York

101   *Rims*, 2005
MDF, wood, steel, paint
112 x 86 x 72 cm (44 x 34 x 28 in)
Private Collection, Birmingham, Alabama
Courtesy MARC FOXX, Los Angeles, and Andrea Rosen Gallery, New York

104   *Obese Eclipsed Cock*, 2005
MDF, Duron, paint
109 x 15 x 254 cm (43 x 6 x 100 in)
Courtesy MARC FOXX, Los Angeles, and Andrea Rosen Gallery, New York

106   *Gate Open*, 2005
MDF, wood, Duron, paint
70 x 186 x 89 cm (27 x 73 x 35 in)
Courtesy MARC FOXX, Los Angeles, and Andrea Rosen Gallery, New York

DRAWINGS

17   a   *Rest and Relaxation*, 2005
Coloured pencil on paper, 28 x 21 cm (11 x 8 in)
Courtesy Vacio 9, Madrid, and Andrea Rosen Gallery, New York

18   b   *Medevac Net*, 2005
Pen on paper, 21 x 28 cm (8 x 11 in)
Courtesy Vacio 9, Madrid, and Andrea Rosen Gallery, New York

18   c   *Even With This Paranoia Inspired Anal Leakage*, 2005
Pastel on paper with collage, 21 x 28 cm (8 x 11 in)
From a four-drawing suite entitled *Oh My God What Are We Gonna Do?!*
Courtesy Vacio 9, Madrid, and Andrea Rosen Gallery, New York

19   d   *Scared To Death Or Learn To Love Cum On Your Face*, 2005
Collage and pastel on paper, 21 x 28 cm (8 x 11 in)
From a four-drawing suite entitled *Oh My God What Are We Gonna Do?!*
Courtesy Vacio 9, Madrid, and Andrea Rosen Gallery, New York

20   e   *We Are Not Raw Materials*, 2005
Pastel on paper, 21 x 28 cm (8 x 11 in)
From a four-drawing suite entitled *Oh My God What Are We Gonna Do?!*
Courtesy Vacio 9, Madrid, and Andrea Rosen Gallery, New York

20   f   *Black Torso*, 2005
Pastel on paper, 21 x 28 cm (8 x 11 in)
Courtesy Vacio 9, Madrid, and Andrea Rosen Gallery, New York

21   g   *Green Zone Without Fence*, 2005
Coloured pencil on paper, 21 x 28 cm (8 x 11 in)
Courtesy Vacio 9, Madrid, and Andrea Rosen Gallery, New York

21   h   *Behind The Bushes*, 2005
Pastel on paper, 21 x 28 cm (8 x 11 in)
Courtesy Vacio 9, Madrid; and Andrea Rosen Gallery, New York

22   i   *Empty Highway*, 2005
Ink on archival paper, 21 x 28 cm (8 x 11 in)
Signature, title, and date verso
Courtesy MARC FOXX, Los Angeles, and Andrea Rosen Gallery, New York

23   j   *Empty Landscape*, 2005
Ink and pastel on archival paper, 21 x 28 cm (8 x 11 in)
Signature, title, and date verso
Courtesy MARC FOXX, Los Angeles, and Andrea Rosen Gallery, New York

24   k1   *Just Someone Who Stopped Watching CNN*, 2005
     k2   *Loosening What's Acceptable*, 2005
     k3   *Hello*, 2005
     k4   *Lost The Desire To Have Kids*, 2005
     k5   *Who Was The Time?*, 2005
     k6   *Hormonal Fog*, 2005
     k7   *Want To Really Do*, 2005
     k8   *Might As Well Cum In The Toilet*, 2005
Ink and pastel on archival paper; each 21 x 28 cm (8 x 11 in)
Signature, title, and date verso
From the nine-drawing suite entitled *Falling... Spilling... Sprawling...*
Courtesy MARC FOXX, Los Angeles, and Andrea Rosen Gallery, New York

25   l   *Cupcake Anal Beads*, 2005
Ink and pastel on archival paper, 21 x 28 cm (8 x 11 in)
From a four-drawing suite entitled *Oh My God What Are We Gonna Do?!*
Courtesy Andrea Rosen Gallery, New York

26   m   *Abstract Expressionism*, 2005
Ink and pastel on archival paper, 21 x 28 cm (8 x 11 in)
Signature, title, and date verso
Courtesy MARC FOXX, Los Angeles, and Andrea Rosen Gallery, New York

26   n   *As In So Fat You Can't See Your Penis*, 2005
Ink and pastel on archival paper, 21 x 28 cm (8 x 11 in)
Signature, title, and date verso
From a six-drawing suite entitled *Shine The Light*
Courtesy MARC FOXX, Los Angeles, and Andrea Rosen Gallery, New York

27   o   *Murdering Thousands Of Potentials*, 2005
Ink and pastel on archival paper, 21 x 28 cm (8 x 11 in)
Signature, title, and date verso
From a six-drawing suite entitled *Shine The Light*
Courtesy MARC FOXX, Los Angeles, and Andrea Rosen Gallery, New York

28   p   *Blood In Stool, Poos In Pool*, 2005
Ink and pastel on archival paper, 21 x 28 cm (8 x 11 in)
Signature, title, and date verso
From a six-drawing suite entitled *Shine The Light*
Courtesy MARC FOXX, Los Angeles, and Andrea Rosen Gallery, New York

29   q   *Red Lacing*, 2005
Ink and pastel on archival paper, 21 x 28 cm (8 x 11 in)
Signature, title, and date verso
From a six-drawing suite entitled *Shine The Light*
Courtesy MARC FOXX, Los Angeles, and Andrea Rosen Gallery, New York

29   r   *Love Stroking It To Your Cut Out B-Hole*, 2005
Ink and pastel on archival paper, 21 x 28 cm (8 x 11 in)
Signature, title, and date verso
From a six-drawing suite entitled *Shine The Light*
Courtesy MARC FOXX, Los Angeles, and Andrea Rosen Gallery, New York

30   s   *People Of The World Unite*, 2006
Pen and pastel on archival paper, 28 x 43 cm (11 x 17 in)
Courtesy Andrea Rosen Gallery, New York

30   t   *The Other Side*, 2006
Pen on archival paper, 28 x 43 cm (11 x 17 in)
Courtesy Andrea Rosen Gallery, New York

31   u   *Police State*, 2006
Pencil on archival paper, 28 x 43 cm (11 x 17 in)
Courtesy Andrea Rosen Gallery, New York

31   v   *In The Saloon*, 2006
Pencil on archival paper, 28 x 43 cm (11 x 17 in)
Courtesy Andrea Rosen Gallery, New York

32   w   *Bloody Tsunami*, 2005
Pen and pastel on archival paper, 21 x 28 cm (8 x 11 in)
Courtesy Andrea Rosen Gallery, New York

32   x   *To Possess It*, 2006
Pen on archival paper, 28 x 43 cm (11 x 17 in)
Courtesy Andrea Rosen Gallery, New York

MATTHEW RONAY

Born 1976, Louisville, Kentucky, USA. Lives and works in Brooklyn, NY

EDUCATION

2000 MFA Yale University, 1998 BFA Maryland Institute College of Art

SOLO EXHIBITIONS

2006
Nils Staerk, Copenhagen, Denmark
MARC FOXX, West Gallery – Project Room, Los Angeles
Parasol unit, London, UK, *Goin' Down, Down, Down: Matthew Ronay*, Sept 12–Nov 8
Vacio 9, Madrid, Spain, *Oh My God What Are We Gonna Do?!* Feb 2–Mar 3

2005
Andrea Rosen Gallery, New York, NY, *It's An Uprising!*
MARC FOXX, Los Angeles, CA, *Shine The Light*
rec./Esther Schipper, Berlin, Germany, *Love Will Find A Way*

2004
Art Statements, presented by Nils Staerk Contemporary Art, Art Basel 35, Switzerland

2002–03
Andrea Rosen Gallery, New York, NY, *Gallery 2: Catarina Leitão & Matthew Ronay*

2002
Nils Staerk, Copenhagen, Denmark

2001
MARC FOXX, Los Angeles, CA

GROUP EXHIBITIONS

2006
SUMMER, Nils Staerk, Copenhagen, Denmark, July 7–Aug 19

2005
Withdrawal, Galerie Chez Valentin, Paris, Feb 26–April 2
Make It Now: New Sculpture in New York, SculptureCenter, Long Island City, NY,
May 15–July 31. (catalogue)
Uncertain States of America. American Art in the 3rd Millennium, Astrup Fearnley
Museum of Modern Art, Oslo, Aug 10–Nov 13. (catalogue) Travelling to: Musee d'Art
Moderne de la Ville de Paris, Paris, Center for Curatorial Studies, Bard College,
Annandale-on-Hudson, New York, Reykjavik Art Museum, Reykjavik, Serpentine Gallery,
London, UK
Monuments for the USA, CCAC Wattis Institute for Contemporary Arts, San Francisco,
CA, April 7–May 14. Travelling to White Columns, New York, NY, Dec 13–Feb 7
The Art of Chess, Luhring Augustine, New York, Oct 28–Dec 23. Travelling to Gary
Tatintsian Gallery, Inc., Moscow, Russia, Apr 13–May 15, 2006. (catalogue)

2004
2004 Whitney Biennial Exhibition, curated by Chrissie Iles, Shamim M. Momin and Debra
Singer, Whitney Museum of American Art, New York, NY, Mar 11–May 30. (catalogue)
the stars are so big, THE EARTH IS SO SMALL... stay as you are (Part I), curated by
Robert Meijer, Esther Schipper Gallery, Berlin, Germany, Sep 10–Oct 16. Travelled to
Studio Manuela Klerkx in Milan, Italy, Mar 17–Apr 8, 2005

2003
<--> *Matthew Ronay, Evan Holloway and Hiroshi Sugito*, MARC FOXX, Los Angeles, CA,
Mar 22–Apr 19
We are electric, curated by Chris Perez, Deitch Projects, New York, NY, Nov 8–Dec 20
Game Over, Grimm Rosenfeld, Munich, Germany, Oct 9–Oct 25
New Slang, Luhring Augustine Gallery, New York, NY

2002
Artists Imagine Architecture, Institute of Contemporary Art, Boston, MA (catalogue)
Group Show, MARC FOXX, Los Angeles, CA
Sudden Glory: Sight Gags and Slapstick in Contemporary Art, Logan Gallery
CCAC Wattis Institute for Contemporary Arts, San Francisco, CA (catalogue)
Now is the Time, Dorsky Gallery Curatorial Programs, Long Island City, NY (catalogue)

2001
Boomerang, Collectors Choice, Exit Art, New York, NY
Group Sculpture Show, MARC FOXX, Los Angeles, CA
Mink Jazz, curated by Bruce Hainley, MARC FOXX, Los Angeles, CA

2000
Two Friends and So On, organized by Rob Pruitt and Jonathan Horowitz, Andrew Kreps
Gallery, New York, NY

1999
Minty, curated by Bruce Hainley, Richard Telles Gallery, Los Angeles, CA

BIBLIOGRAPHY

2006
Morton, Tom, 'Uncertain States of America', *Frieze*, March, p. 159

2005
Stosuy, Brandon, 'Matthew Ronay', *The Believer*, Dec 2005/Jan 2006
Danto, Arthur C, 'Uncertain States of America', *Artforum*, December, p. 274
Mack, Joshua, 'Emerging Artists: Matthew Ronay, *Joshua Mack on the dangers of
overeating*', *Modern Painters*, December, pp. 62, 63
'Future Greats', *Art Review*, December, p. 80
Sholis, Brian, 'Reviews: Matthew Ronay', *Artforum*, Summer Issue, p. 324
Scott, Andrea K, '*The new new things*', *Time Out New York*, June 2–8, p. 73
Menelsohn, Adam E., 'Debut: *Discovering emerging artists*, Matthew Ronay', *Art
Review*, May, p. 100
Comer-Greene, Rachel, 'Matthew Ronay, It's an Uprising!', *Time Out New York*,
Mar 10–16, p. 76
Smith, Roberta, 'Matthew Ronay: It's an Uprising', *The New York Times*, Mar 18, p. E42

2004
Weyland, Jocko, 'American Splendor', *Time Out New York*, Mar 4–11, pp. 14–15
Brake, Alan, 'Super-Realist Supreme', *Louisville Magazine*, Apr, pp. 49–50
Kimmelman, Michael. 'Touching All Bases At The Biennial', *The New York Times*, Mar 12, p. E27

2002
Cotter, Holland, 'Architectural Visions Keep Dreamers Awake', *The New York Times*, July 12, p. B37
Kinsella, Eileen, 'Wise Buys: Experts suggest great values in today's market', *Artnews*, Summer Issue
Mondt, Zoey, 'Matthew Ronay at Marc Foxx Gallery', *Frieze*, April, p. 100
Pagel, David, 'Matthew Ronay's Miniature Stage Sets', *Los Angeles Times*, Jan 18, p. F41

EXHIBITION CATALOGUES

2006
de Weck Ardalan, Ziba; Glover, Michael; Hainley, Bruce, *Goin' Down, Down, Down: Matthew Ronay*. London: Parasol unit. Zurich: JRP|Ringier

2005
Huberman, Anthony, *Make It Now: New Sculpture in New York*, SculptureCenter, New York
Birnbaum, Daniel; Kvaran, Gunnar B; Obrist, Hans Ulrich; Funcke, Bettina; Kelsey, John; Moreno, Gean; Stark, Frances; Tumlir, Jan; Turner, Elisa, *Uncertain States of America*, Astrup Fearnley Museum of Modern Art, Oslo, Norway
Rugoff, Ralph, *Monuments for the USA*, CCAC Wattis Institute for Contemporary Arts, San Francisco
Pukemova, Victoria, *The Art of Chess*, Gary Tatintsian Gallery, Inc., Moscow. Russia

2004
Iles, Chrissie; Momin, Shamim M.; Singer, Debra, *Whitney Biennial 2004*, Whitney Museum of American Art, New York

2002
Morgan, Jessica, *Artists Imagine Architecture*, The Institute of Contemporary Art, Boston, MA
Rugoff, Ralph, *Sudden Glory*, CCAC Wattis Institute for Contemporary Arts, San Francisco, CA

BOOKS

Robert Klanten and Sven Ehmann, Editors, *Hidden Track, How Visual Culture Is Going Places*, Berlin: Die Gestalten Verlag, 2005

Published by Parasol unit foundation for contemporary art
on the occasion of the exhibition *Goin' Down, Down, Down: Matthew Ronay*
12 September–9 December 2006

Editor: Ziba de Weck Ardalan for Parasol unit foundation for contemporary art, London
Editing and copyediting: Helen Wire
Book concept and design: moiré, Marc Kappeler, Markus Reichenbach, Zurich
Photography: Christopher Burke (pp. 54–77), Rob Kassabian (pp. 80–87),
Robert Wedemeyer (pp. 90–107)
Cover: Detail from *Officer, Officer, Officer, Officer!*, 2005. Courtesy Andrea Rosen
Gallery, NY
Typeface: UnicaSB
Paper: Ikonogloss 170 g/m^2, PlanoPak 60 g/m^2
Printed in Switzerland by Druckerei Odermatt, Dallenwil
Binding by Schumacher AG, Schmitten

Parasol unit foundation for contemporary art
14 Wharf Road, London N1 7RW
T +44 (0)20 7490 7373, F +44 (0)20 7490 7775
E info@parasol-unit.org, www.parasol-unit.org

jrp|ringier

Distributed by JRP|Ringier
Letzigraben 134, CH-8047 Zurich
T +41 (0)43 311 27 50, F +41 (0)43 311 27 51
E info@jrp-ringier.com, www.jrp-ringier.com

ISBN 10: 3-905770-12-1
ISBN 13: 978-3-905770-12-4

JRP|Ringier books are available internationally at selected bookstores and the following
distribution partners:

Switzerland: Buch 2000, AVA Verlagsauslieferung AG, Centralweg 16,
CH-8910 Affoltern a.A., buch2000@ava.ch
France: Les Presses du réel, 16 rue Quentin, F-21000 Dijon, info@lespressesdureel.com
Germany and Austria: Vice Versa Vertrieb, Immanuelkirchstrasse 12, D-10405 Berlin,
info@vice-versa-vertrieb.de
UK: Art Data, 12 Bell Industrial Estate, 50 Cunnington Street, GB-London W4 5HB,
info@artdata.co.uk
USA: D.A.P./Distributed Art Publishers, 155 Sixth Avenue, 2nd Floor, USA-New York,
NY 10013, dap@dapinc.com
Other countries: IDEA Books, Nieuwe Herengracht 11, NL-1011 RK Amsterdam,
idea@ideabooks.nl